New York Guitar Method
Primer
Ensemble Book Two

By
Bruce Arnold

I0081508

Muse Eek Publishing Company
New York, New York

Copyright © 2004 by Muse Eek Publishing Company. All rights reserved

ISBN 1-59489-914-2

No part of this publication may be reproduced, stored in a
retrieval system, or transmitted, in any form or by any means,
electronic, mechanical, photocopying, recording, or otherwise,
without the prior written permission of the publisher.

Printed in the United States

This publication can be purchased from your local bookstore or by contacting:
Muse Eek Publishing Company
P.O. Box 509
New York, NY 10276, USA
Phone: 212-473-7030
Fax: 212-473-4601
http://www.muse-eek.com
sales@muse-eek.com

Table Of Contents

Acknowledgments

The author would like to thank Gabriel Cummins for his many hours of help in putting this latest series of books together.   I would also like to thank Michal Shapiro for proof reading and helpful suggestions and finally Ronald Andryshak for his administrative assistance.

About the Author

Born in Sioux Falls South Dakota, Bruce Arnold began his music training at the University of South Dakota. After three years of study he transferred to the Berklee College of Music where he received a Bachelor of Music degree in Composition. While doing undergraduate work at Berklee College of Music Bruce received the Harris Stanton award for outstanding guitarist of the year. He continued with further study in improvisational and compositional methods with Charlie Banacos and Jerry Bergonzi. Bruce received the outstanding teacher of the year award at Berklee in 1984 and went on to teach at the New England Conservatory of Music, and Dartmouth College.

Upon moving to New York City, Bruce found himself preoccupied with the possibilities of applying the twelve tone theoretical constructs of Schoenberg and Berg to American improvised music. His first CD, Blue Eleven contained the seeds of those ideas he was to develop further in his following critically acclaimed works: "A Few Dozen" and "Give 'Em Some." In this vein, his music is remarkably tonal, and the results give proof that inventive improvisation is possible within this format.

Bruce currently plays with his own band, "The Bruce Arnold Trio" and with "Spooky Actions" a jazz quartet that performs his transcriptions of Webern and other classical masters. In addition, Bruce has performed with such diverse musicians as Gary Burton, Joe Pass, Joe Lovano, Randy Brecker, Peter Erskine, Stuart Hamm, Boston Symphony Orchestra, and The Absolute Ensemble under the baton of Kristjan Järvi.

Bruce currently teaches at Princeton University, New York University and the New School. Upon his arrival at NYU he set about to improve the music education program, and instituted NYU's first sight-reading program for jazz guitarists. He started writing music education books to fill a need he perceived in formal jazz education.

As an author, Bruce has written 50 books on music education. These books cover many of the important aspects of mastering high performance skills for both the advanced music student with professional goals, and the dedicated beginner. To view the complete catalogue, please log on to his publisher's website at: http://www.muse-eek.com.

Foreword

The New York Guitar Method series is structured for a total beginner to learn the tools necessary to become a master musician from the ground up. This Primer Ensemble Book Two should be used in conjunction with New York Guitar Method Primer Book Two. Both books are prerequisites for students entering NYU as a jazz guitar major and for students wishing to go to the New York Guitar Summer Program at NYU. There is a developing online resource including midifiles and FAQs that can be found on the title page of the muse-eek.com website. You will also find additional help files in the member's area.

If you are a beginner with little experience reading music I recommend you start with New York Guitar Method Primer Book 1.

Bruce Arnold

New York, New York

How To Use This Book

The purpose of this book is to improve your sight reading skills. Each chapter is broken down into several sections to help isolate the many challenging areas of this topic.

The first and perhaps most important aspect of sight reading is reading rhythm. Chapter One includes a complete description for understanding rhythmic notation. Each chapter contains three rhythm exercises. The goal for these exercises is to familiarize your eye with the many different combinations of rhythm you will encounter. You want to be able to read those rhythms as quickly and accurately as possible. Directions for these exercises which include goal tempos can be found on page 23.

The next exercises are single string studies. The goal of these exercises is to get you reading on one string the entire length of the neck without having to look down to see where your hand is. It usually takes a student at least six month to become comfortable reading these exercises but the reward is invaluable: you will know where every note occurs on the entire length of each string and you will never again have to look at your hands to find a note on the fretboard.

The rhythm changes exercises in this book serve a dual purpose. Reading these lines at extremely fast tempos will get your eye accustomed to the kind of reading you might encounter in up tempo big band charts. These exercises are also great material for part reading in a guitar ensemble.

The last section in each chapter consists of a modal vamp and a solo to go along with the vamp. The vamps which take a short modal progression through twelve keys are a great resource for working on commonly used comping rhythms and voicings. The solos will challenge your ability to read single note melodies and will increase your rhythmic and melodic vocabulary in the jazz idiom. Included at the end of each solo is a description of the improvisational techniques used throughout the example. You should read these descriptions and then review the solo as they can open the door for understanding how great improvisers use techniques like modal sequencing and approach notes.

Directions for all these exercises including tempo suggestions can be found on page 23.

A word to the wise

I'd like to say a few words about how I believe a student should approach being a musician, a guitarist and an artist.

The first thing that comes to mind is the old joke:
Q: How many guitarists does it take to change a light bulb?
A: Two, one to change it and one to say they could have done it better.

Competitiveness in music is both destructive to the musical community and to the accused and the accuser. Each person projects their own voice through their instrument. Granted this voice can be anywhere from weak and ineffective to revolutionary and technically astounding. The important thing to realize is that all great musicians were once weak and ineffective. It is dedication, knowing the right thing to practice and artistic vision that eventually makes a musician great. Closely related to this is the common argument that this guitarist is better than that guitarist. This is such an absurd line of thought. Who is better; Django Reinheirt or Charley Christian? —Pat Metheny or John Scofield? Obviously they all have brought their own unique language to music and one is not "greater" than the other. Therefore look for the uniqueness in a guitarist and remember their voice may be only just beginning to emerge. And of course, all musical taste is <u>subjective</u>. Keep in mind that you might not like music which is very good, and like music that other people simply cannot relate to. Remember that an opinion is not a fact.

Secondly I'd like to make some comments about being a student. While respect for your teacher is a given, the best and most effective student is one who thinks on their own and questions both their preconceptions and the information their teachers give them. The worst thing you can do is just figure "my teacher plays better than me, therefore I should do everything he or she says without questioning it's validity." This doesn't mean you have to enter into a contentious relationship with your teacher, it means you need to think logically about what they are asking you to do and ask honest questions if you are uncertain that their advice is the best. Another common mistake I see among students is thinking that studying with the most famous person will net them the best information and therefore they will achieve their goals more quickly. Someone's ability on their instrument and certainly their popularity doesn't make them a good teacher. A good teacher is above all someone who cares whether you improve and then has the insights to convey assignments tailored to your needs along with a deep understanding of all aspects of working towards mastering an instrument. This is usually a rare commodity and isn't something that is automatically inherent in a musician that is famous.

Third. Be a buddy. Jon Damien, a great teacher at Berklee College of Music had a buddy system he promoted there. It's such a simple concept, but it can lay the foundations for the right attitude towards practice and interaction with the other members of your musical community. <u>And that's as crucial as any other part of your development.</u> Here's the concept: Seek out other guitarists to play and practice with. This will help you develop and let you see other musical possibilities through your buddy's eyes and ears. It will also help you build a community of people that may even eventually of people that may even eventually support you in your career. This very closely relates back to the first point I made. It's important to keep yourself open and nonjudgmental. Remember you don't want to play only with someone you feel is more developed than you. Someone not quite as developed as you in the ways you currently feel are important may have other aspects of their playing that could influence you positively. Look for the strong points in your fellow musicians and learn from them.

Fourth and unfortunately too common with guitarist is the notion that fast equals good. Anyone can tell if someone is playing fast—that's not even something you need to be a musician to do. Someone who bases their analysis of a musician on their technique is someone who doesn't understand first what art is and secondly what good music is. Your evaluation of a musician should be based on whether this person has an affinity with your artistic vision and says something through their instrument that touches you in a deeper way. In conjunction with this remember your artistic vision is always a work in progress so your analysis has to be always tempered by the fact that someone's playing may not mean something to you at your current state of development, but may speak to you later on.

Lastly a few tidbits of advice:

Try not to tell another musician that their music or playing sounds like "X" person. A true artist is trying as hard as they can to find their own personal sound, so this kind of statement is not what they really want to hear. You will most likely get an unenthusiastic "thank you" and a glazed look. Keep in mind that your current state of development might be telling you that they sound like someone else but later on you may find that they have something unique to offer.

It's good to have heroes, and to emulate the way that they play, but you are who you are, and you should not start out trying to sound like anyone else. Each day try to find something in your practicing that can define your voice. This can start with the smallest thing but can grow into a singular vision.

What works for one person may not work for another. If you have a good teacher, your assignments will be tailor made for you, and would not necessarily be relevant for another student. The converse is true—what another person is working on may not have any value for you.

Just because someone famous has a lack of knowledge of music theory and sight reading doesn't mean that you should follow in their footsteps. The requirements of a musician's success change over time along with the era in which they may have gotten their greatest career boost. Things are a lot more demanding these days, and you would be best served to have all the "tools of the trade" at your command when you assail the walls of professional music.

Chapter One

Rhythm Explanation

Directions For Sight Reading Exercises

Rhythm Exercise

Single String Exercise

Rhythm Changes Exercise

Modal Jazz Vamp and Solo

Understanding Rhythm Notation

The rhythm in a piece of music is presented in overall units called "measures." These measures are further divided up into beats. (More on this in a moment) Example One shows you one "measure" of music. There are many different symbols in a measure of music. These symbols show how to play the music. To the far left there is always a clef sign. This tells the reader what pitch level the notes will be on the staff. The clef sign used here is the treble clef sign, therefore the 4 notes presented in this measure would be four middle C's. The next symbol is the time signature. This tells you how the measure will be divided rhythmically. In this case the time signature is 4/4. The top 4 tells you how many beats are in a measure. In this case the measure has 4 beats in it. The bottom 4 tells you what unit of measure will be used to show those 4 beats. In this case the 4 represents a quarter note. So this whole measure is divided up into 4 quarters and these 4 quarters are each represented by a note called a quarter note. A quarter note would be held for one beat. A line is placed at the end of each measure to show where the end of each measure is.

Example 1

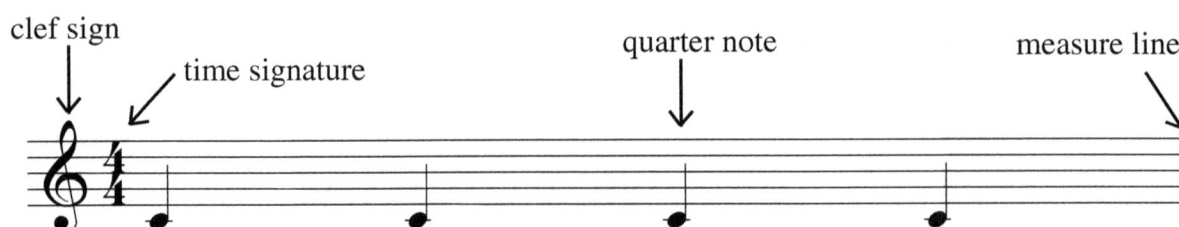

Rhythm can of course be much more or less complicated than example 1. In example 2 we still have a 4/4 measure and it still has only 4 beats in the measure but we have only one note which happens on beat one. This note takes up all four beats of the measure so you would sustain the sound for four beats. This note is called a whole note. Example 3 shows a measure that has been divided up into two equal parts. These notes are called half notes and because we have a 4/4 measure there can only be 2 half notes in a measure because a half note gets 2 beats. The first note is played on beat one and the second note is played on beat 3.

Example 2

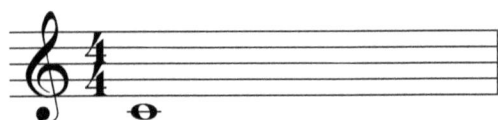

Example 3

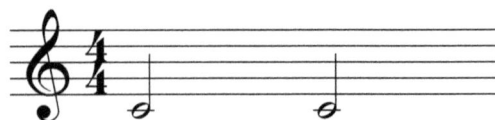

As I have said, rhythm can be much more complicated than the previous example. In example 4 we still have a 4/4 measure and it still has only 4 beats in the measure but each beat has been divided into equal divisions to form a new rhythm. So now rather than just four rhythmic hits in the measure there are eight. These new notes are referred to as eighth notes because it takes 8 eighth notes to make up one measure of 4/4. So for each beat you would play two notes equally dividing that beat into two parts.

Example 4

Rhythm can be further subdivided. In example 5 each beat has been subdivided into three equal parts. These three note groups are commonly called triplets and usually have a bracket and a number three placed above the grouping. Therefore you would play three notes for each beat equally dividing that beat into three parts.

Example 5

We can also divide each beat into 4 equal parts. In example 6 each beat has been subdivided into four equal parts. Each note of this four note grouping is called a sixteenth note. Therefore you would play four notes for each beat, equally dividing that beat into four parts.

Example 6

We can also divide each beat into eight equal parts. In example 7 each beat has been subdivided into 8 equal parts. Each note of this eight note grouping is called a thirty second note. Therefore you would play eight notes for each beat equally dividing that beat into eight parts.

Example 7

Rests

Each of the rhythms presented in the previous seven examples could leave some notes out to create other rhythms. These left out notes are called rests and use the symbols shown below. During the rests you don't play anything. You will see in the forthcoming examples that when rests are placed into measures the rhythm can become quite complex. We will start with some simple examples.

Examples 8-10 show measures with three kinds of rests. In example 8 there is a whole note rest. Nothing would be played during this measure. Example 9 shows a half note rest. In this case nothing would be played for the first two beats of the measure. Example 10 shows a quarter note rest. In this case nothing would be played for beat 3 of this measure.

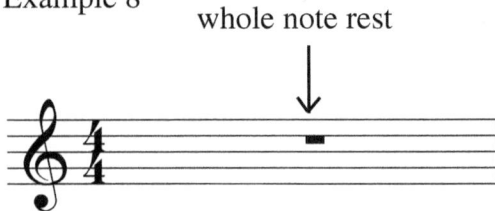

Example 8   whole note rest

Example 9   half note rest

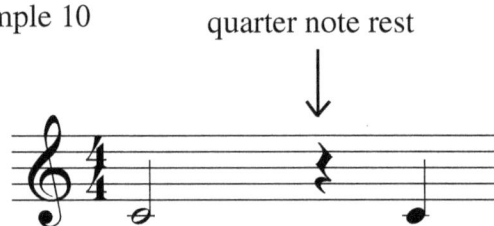

Example 10   quarter note rest

Examples 11-12 show measures that are composed of eighth notes but in which some of the eighth notes have been left out.

Example 11   eighth note rest

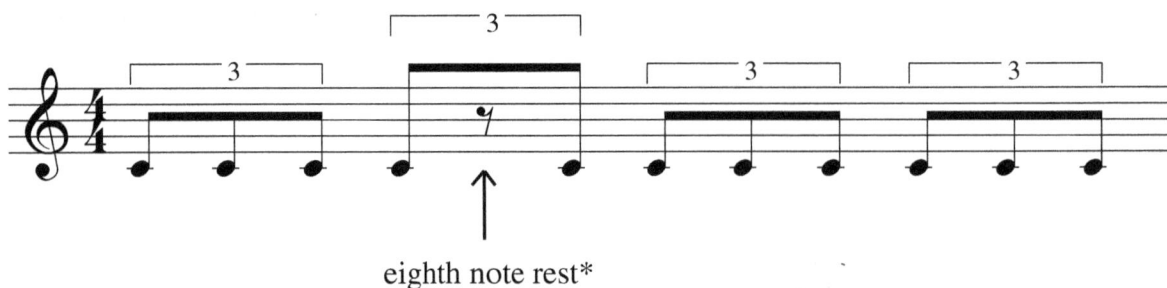

Example 12

eighth note rest*

*Note: Eighth notes within a triplet receive 1/3 of a beat. Therefore when an eighth note rest is found within a triplet the eighth note rest equals 1/3 of a beat.

Example 13 shows you a sixteenth note rhythm where a sixteenth note rest has been added.

Example 13

sixteenth note rest

Example 14 shows you a thirty second note rhythm where a thirty second note rest has been added.

Example 14

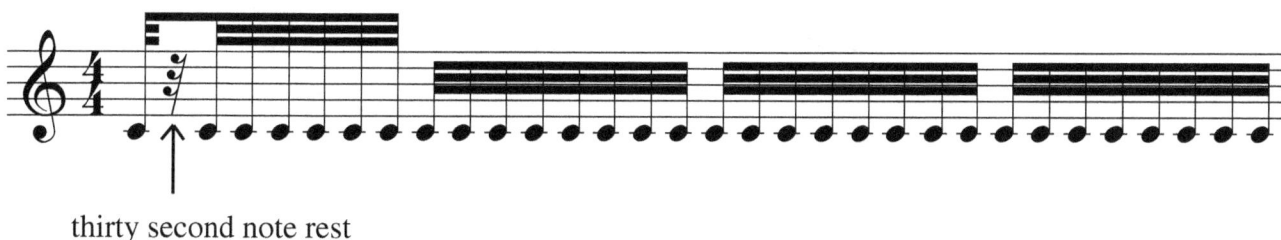

thirty second note rest

A measure can contain a variety of rests. Example 15 shows you a measure with various types of rests.

Example 15

* A sixteenth note is written with two *flags* on its right side to indicate its value when found alone.

Dots

A dot can be placed after a note or rest to lengthen its value. A dot adds 1/2 of the note's value, therefore in example 16, the dot placed after the eighth note rest adds a one sixteenth rest, totalling a rest of three sixteenths. (One eighth plus one sixteenth = 3 sixteenths.) Example 17 shows the same situation but with a note rather than a rest.

Example 16

dot

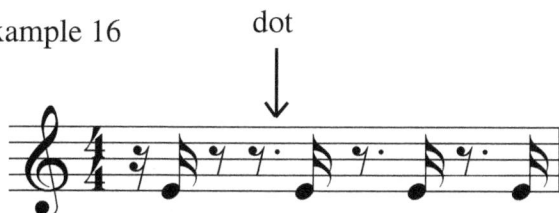

Example 17

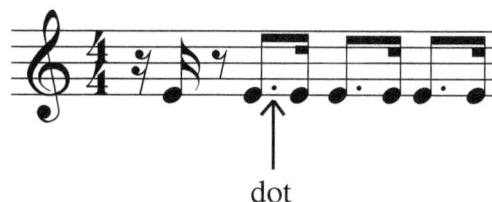

dot

Ties

Ties can also be placed into music to lengthen a particular note. Example 18 shows two quarter notes tied together. Example 19 shows what this rhythm would sound like.

Example 18

Example 19

Counting

Although I don't recommend it as a long term habit, a beginner often needs a method to help count each beat and subdivision. Over time you should develop the ability to recognize any rhythm and know what it sounds like. But again, if you are a beginner or you are having a problem with a rhythm, counting is a way to work it through. The follow examples give the counting method I recommend.

Understanding Triplets

Please note before reading this section that there are not many triplet rhythms used for the musical examples in this book. However, in order to gain a complete understanding of rhythm and to ensure your success in the future volumns in this series I highly reccomend you read this section on triplets.

Now that you have a basic understanding of how to read and understand rhythm let's take a more in-depth look at triplets. You will find triplet rhythms in almost all of the rhythm primer exercises in this book. It is important that you understand how to play these rhythms. You will find that listening to the midifiles found on the muse-eek.com website will help you to hear how the triplet rhythms sound.

The next pages deal with how to count and understand triplets. Make sure to listen to each example, because when you hear these triplets you will often find that the rhythm looks a lot harder than it really is.

Triplets divide a beat into three equal parts. In example 1, each beat has been subdivided into three equal parts. These three note groups are commonly called triplets and usually have a bracket and a number three placed above the grouping. Therefore you would play three notes for each beat equally dividing that beat into three parts. To play this example tap your right hand three times for each tap of your foot. Your right hand is playing the triplets and your foot is counting out the 4 beats of a 4/4 measure of music.

Example 1

Although I don't recommend it as a long term habit, a beginner often needs a method for counting each beat and subdivision. Over time you should develop the ability to recognize any rhythm and know what it sounds like. But again, if you are a beginner or you are having a problem with a rhythm, counting is a way to work it through. Example 2 gives the counting method I recommend.

Example 2

Triplets can also be found stretching over more than one beat. This can be very difficult for a beginning student to feel, especially when the tempo is slow. In example 3 we have two quarter note triplet patterns. Each quarter note triplet occupies two beats of the measure. These two beats are divided equally into three equal parts.

Example 3

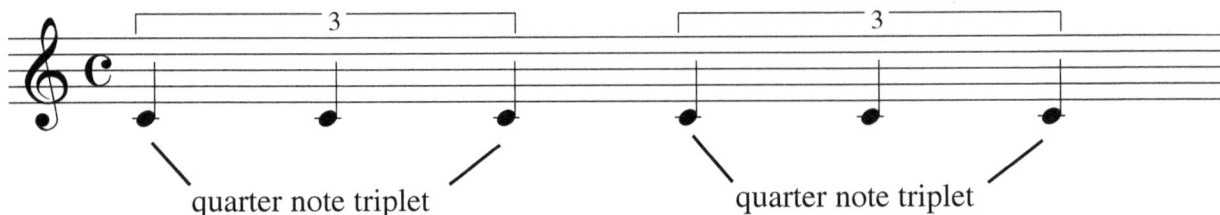

quarter note triplet   quarter note triplet

Sometimes it helps a beginning student to subdivide each beat in a measure in order to hear quarter note triplets. Example 4 is the same rhythm as example 3. The only difference is we have tied the notes of the triplet together in order to make it easier to see the rhythm. Many times writing a pattern in this manner helps a student to see exactly which notes are being played in the quarter note triplet. Notice the following aspects:

    a. The 1st note of the triplet in beat one is tied to the second
    b. The 3rd note of the first triplet is tied to the 1st note of the triplet of beat 2
    c. The 2nd note of beat 2 is tied to the 3rd note of the triplet

This process repeats itself for beats 3 and 4.

Example 4

a.   b.   c.   a.   b.   c.

Example 5 shows you again the relationship between these two ways of writing quarter note triplets.

Example 5

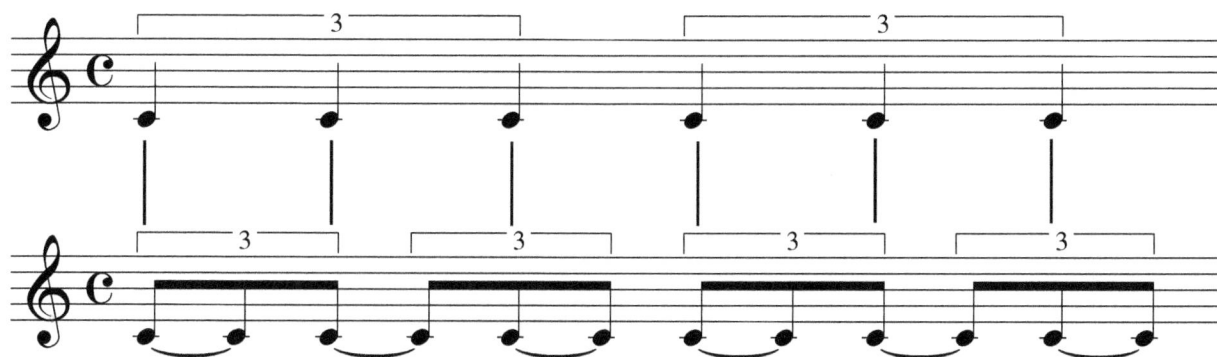

Playing this rhythm is a four step process.

1. Tap your foot on every beat
2. Tap your foot on each beat and say out loud each triplet as shown in example 2
3. Tap the triplets with your right hand while continuing to do step one and two
4. Tap only the 1st and 3rd parts of the triplet in beat one and the 2nd part of the triplet in beat two while continuing to do step one and two

You are now tapping quarter note triplets with your right hand. Continue this process so you can tap the quarter note triplets for beats 3 and 4 too. It will take some time before this is ingrained. I recommend doing this for 5 to 10 minutes a day for a couple of weeks and you should find that you are feeling quarter note triplets naturally.

Half note triplets are another rhythm commonly found in music. Half note triplets divide a 4/4 measure into 3 equal parts. Example 6 shows you a half note triplet.

Example 6

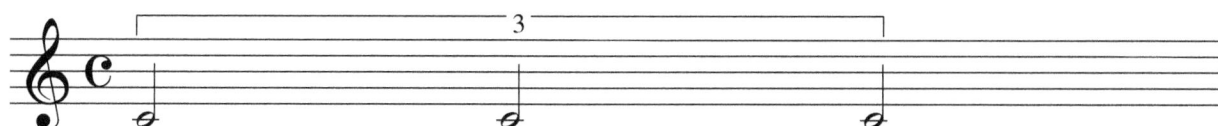

19

The same process of subdividing the measure will help you to see and feel a half note triplet. Example 7 is the same rhythm as example 6. The only difference is that we have tied the notes of the triplet together in order to make it easier to see the rhythm. Once again, writing a half note triplet in this manner will help you to see and feel the rhythm. Notice the following aspects:

     a. The 1st note of the quarter note triplet is tied to the second
     b. The 3rd note of the first quarter note triplet is tied to the 1st note of the second quarter note triplet
     c. The 2nd note of the second quarter note triplet is tied to the 3rd note of the quarter note triplet

Example 7

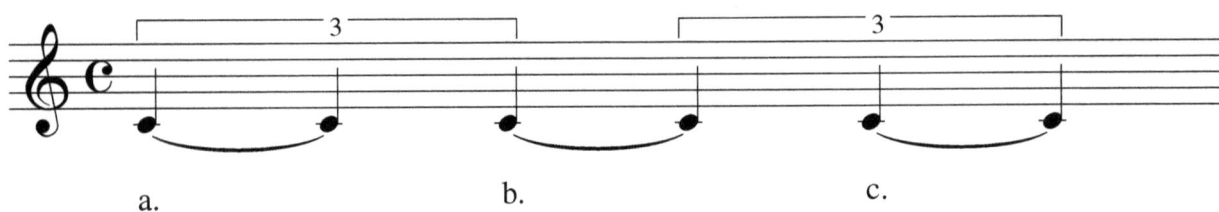

     a.   b.   c.

Example 8 shows you again the relationship between these two ways of writing a half note triplet.

Example 8

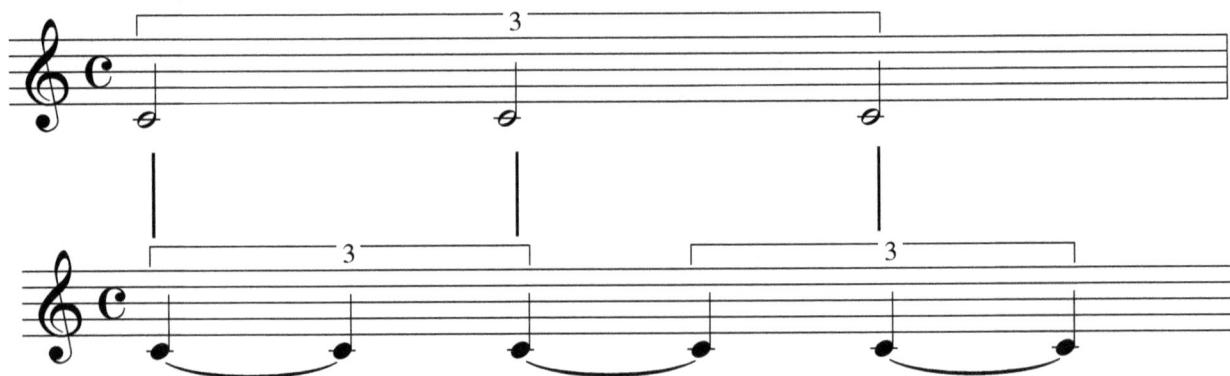

Once again this is a four step process in playing half note triplets.

1. Tap your foot on beats one and three of a 4/4 measure
2. Tap your foot on beats one and three and say out loud each quarter note triplet as shown in example 9

Example 9

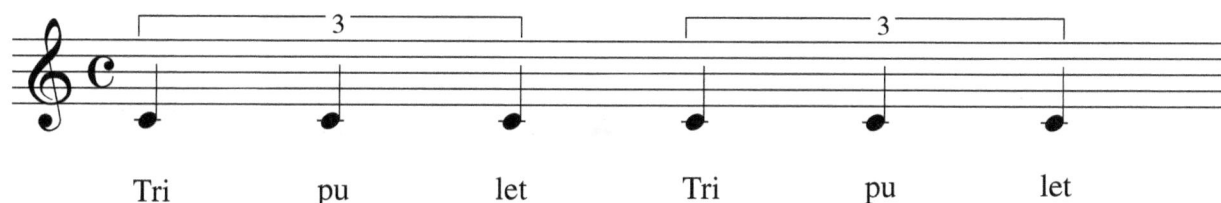

Tri   pu   let   Tri   pu   let

3. Tap the triplets with your right hand while continuing to do step one and two
4. Tap only the 1st and 3rd parts of the quarter note triplet in beat one and the 2nd part of the second quarter note triplet. Example 10 shows you the rhythm you are now tapping.

Example 10

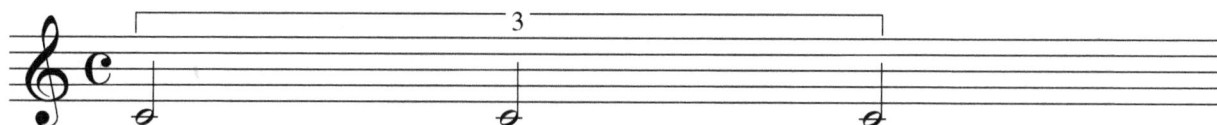

Now that you are tapping half note triplets with your right hand you should continue this process so you can tap the quarter note triplets for beats 3 and 4 too. Again, it will take some time before this is ingrained. I recommend doing this for 5 to 10 minutes a day for a couple of weeks and you should find you are feeling half note triplets naturally.

Some interesting side notes to this process of learning triplets: Usually a student finds the faster they play triplets the easier they are to hear. This is particularly true of half note triplets where if your tap you foot once for a whole measure you only have to divide each tap of the foot into three equal beats with your hand or voice to create half note triplets. Experiment around with different tempos to help you feel triplets in many different ways.

Straight Eighth vs. Swing Eighth Note Feel

       Different styles of music interpret the written eighth note in various ways. Rock and Latin music in general play written music "as written," in other words you just play the notes as you see them.* On the other hand with a "swing feel" which is commonly found in jazz and blues, you play the eighth note with more of a triplet feel. If you have a measure of eighth notes as in (example 1) you would play these eighth notes like a triplet but leaving out the middle note. (See example 2.)

Example 1

Example 2

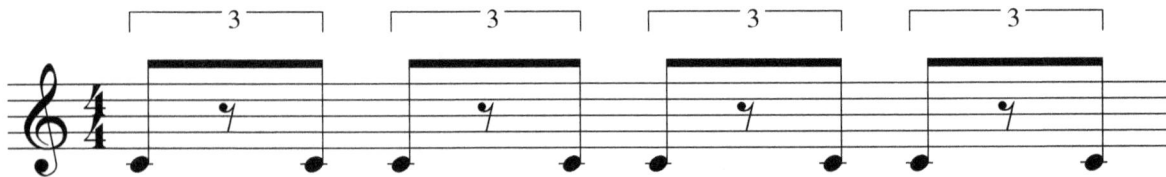

       * There are slight variations among all performers and styles as far as note interpretation goes. It should be kept in mind that examples 1 and 2 are only approximations of how eighth notes are played. Upon closer analysis you will find slight differences between any two styles of interpretation. It is recommended that you transcibe and learn melodies and solos of great jazz, rock and blues players to experience these differences first hand.

Rhythmic Notation

Slanted lines or Slashes

This book uses rhythmic notation which is commonly used in professional music to indicate the rhythm of a chord progression or to "mark" time. Example A shows slanted lines or slashes "/" to indicate each beat in the measure. Example A is in 4/4 time which is also known as common time. This is why there is a "C" shown after the treble clef sign. The slashes are not telling you to play on every beat they are more used for your eye to quickly see how many beats are in each bar or measure.

Example A

4/4 common time

B-   B-   A   A

┌── One bar ──┐

treble clef sign   Slashes showing each beat

When playing a song you very often need to play chords. These chords will be played in a certain rhythm which will help give the song it's distinctive flavor or style. Professional musicians use a specific system of rhythmic notation to indicate the rhythm needed for each chord. Example B shows each chord being played twice per measure and changing chords each measure. You need to play the chords once on the 1st beat and once on the 3rd beat. Rhythmic notation uses similiar types of notes to regular notation. (Please see the member's area of the muse-eek.com website for the help file on rhythm to understand each rhythmic value and how this is notated). You will notice that the diamond shapes with flags look a lot like half notes in regular notation and in fact they have the same value. So for each of the diamond shapes below you will strum the chord which will create two strums per bar on beats one and three.

Example B

G   D   A-   A-
diamond shapes   Beat one   Beat three

flags

All rhythms can be notated with rhythmic notation. Example C shows three of these rhythms. The first bar is a whole note written in rhythmic notation so you strum the chord once. The second measure has a dotted quarter written in rhythmic notation so you play the chord on one and hold it for a beat and half. Next you have an eighth tied to a half note written in rhythmic notation which means you will strum the B♭ chord on two "and"and hold it for 2 and one half beats.

Example C

D-   C   B♭   A

Whole Note
equals 4 beats   Dotted quarter equals   Eighth tied to a half equals
                        one beat and a half   two and one half beats.

23

Beat Reading

If you want to make a significant leap in reading music you need to train your eye to read ahead of the music as it is happening in real time. The beat reading exercise presented here is like speed reading for music. This technique will make an incredible change in your reading ability in a very short amount of time.

I would suggest you practice this method using many different types of music. I would further suggest you use the resources of your local library and their interlibrary loan program which will allow you to get just about any music book that is commercially available. It is important to use a wide variety of music including: classical, jazz, transcribed solos, and music for instruments other than your own. Make sure to choose music from all periods; from Gregorian chant to 20th century classical music to rock. Your eye needs to become familiar with many different types of manuscripts. Furthermore different styles of music have their own idiosyncratic features which need to be mastered in order for you to become a great sight reader. Reading music from all periods and styles will also improve your recognition of different note combinations, rhythms, phrasing and feel.

Practice the following exercises about 10 minutes a day using various music manuscripts.

1 Read only the notes on beat one of each measure.
  If you have a tie from a previous measure or a rest don't play anything.

2. Read only the notes on beat one and three of each measure.
   If you have a tie from a previous note, measure, or a rest don't play anything.

3. Read only the notes on every beat.
   If you have a tie from a previous note, measure, or a rest don't play anything.

Directions for Sight Reading Exercises

Rhythm Primer Exercises

Play each page at whole note = 40. The metronome should click only on beat one. Work your way up to whole note = 120. Play both as a straight eighth feel and a swing feel on the eigth note examples. See page 20 for an explanation of eighth vs. swing feels. There are also downloadable midifiles available at the muse-eek.com website to help you with these exercises.

Single String Exercises

When you work on the example found in this book do not look at your guitar to find the pitch. One of the main ideas of these exercises is to get you to know where a note is by feel and not by looking at the fretboard. I recommend playing these exercises with a low single note drone for each key. For example if you are in C major record a repeating low C note and use your ear to help you confirm if you are playing the right pitch. These exercises should be played quite slowly to begin with.

Rhythm Changes Exercises

The rhythm changes exercises in this book should be read as written and 8va (an octave above the written note). You should start at half note = 60 and work your way up to half note = 120. While playing the exercises in this book the metronome should click on beats 2 and 4 to set up a backbeat swing feel. These exercises can also be played together in an ensemble setting.

Vamps and Solos

In each chapter you are presented with a modal vamp and a solo that corresponds to the mode you are learning in each chapter of New York Guitar Method Primer Book Two. You should pay close attention to playing each vamp with the correct right hand rhythm which is presented in each example. While playing the exercises in this book the metronome should click on beats 2 and 4 to set up a backbeat swing feel. Also, after reading the solo make note of the information that is presented at the end of each exercise on the content and improvisational ideas used in each solo.

I highly recommend practicing these exercises with another guitarist. You could start off reading the vamp while your partner reads the solo and then switch parts.

Rhythm Primer Exercise 1

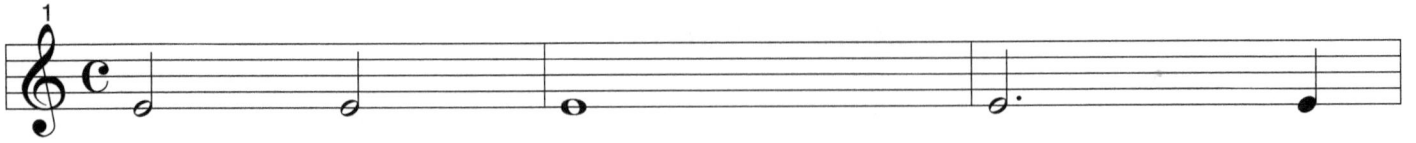

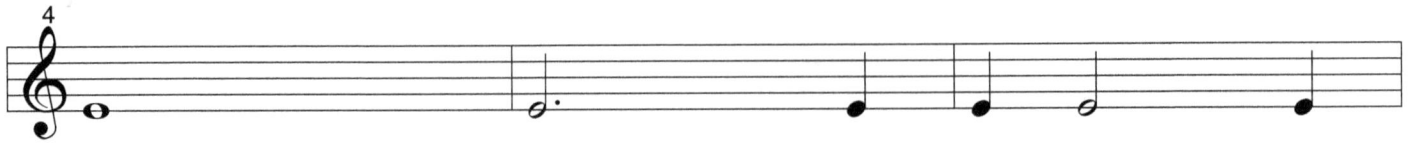

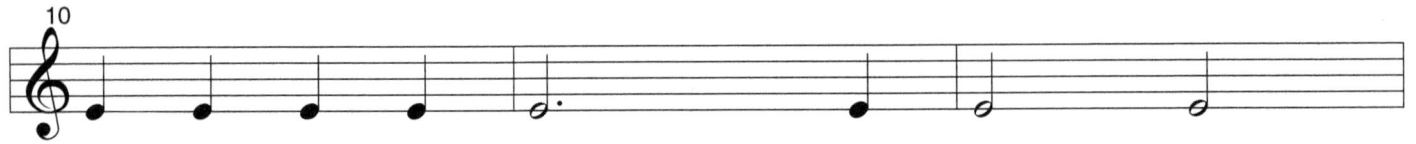

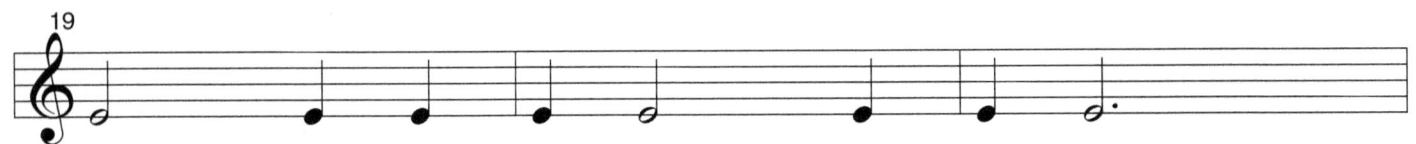

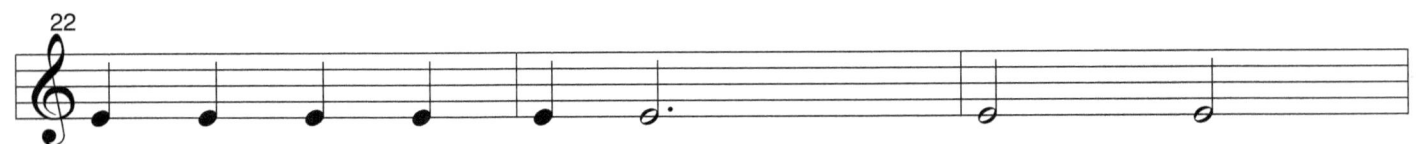

SINGLE STRING EXERCISE 1

TREBLE CLEF

Low E String Only

Key of C Major

C Rhythm Changes Part 1

C Rhythm Changes Part 2

C Rhythm Changes Part 3

C Rhythm Changes Part 4

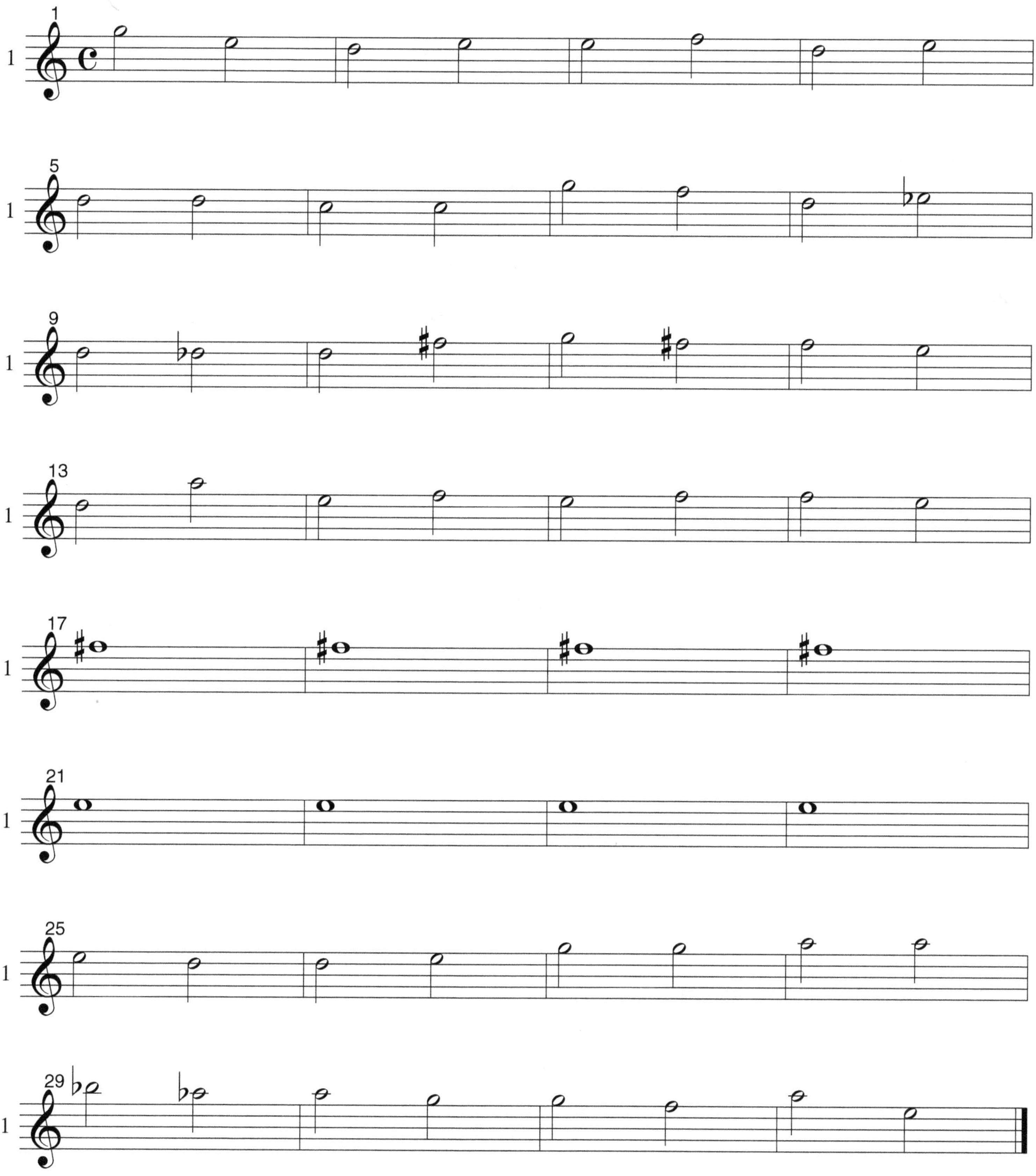

⊓ = Strum with a downward motion

V = Strum with an upward motion

Ionian Vamp

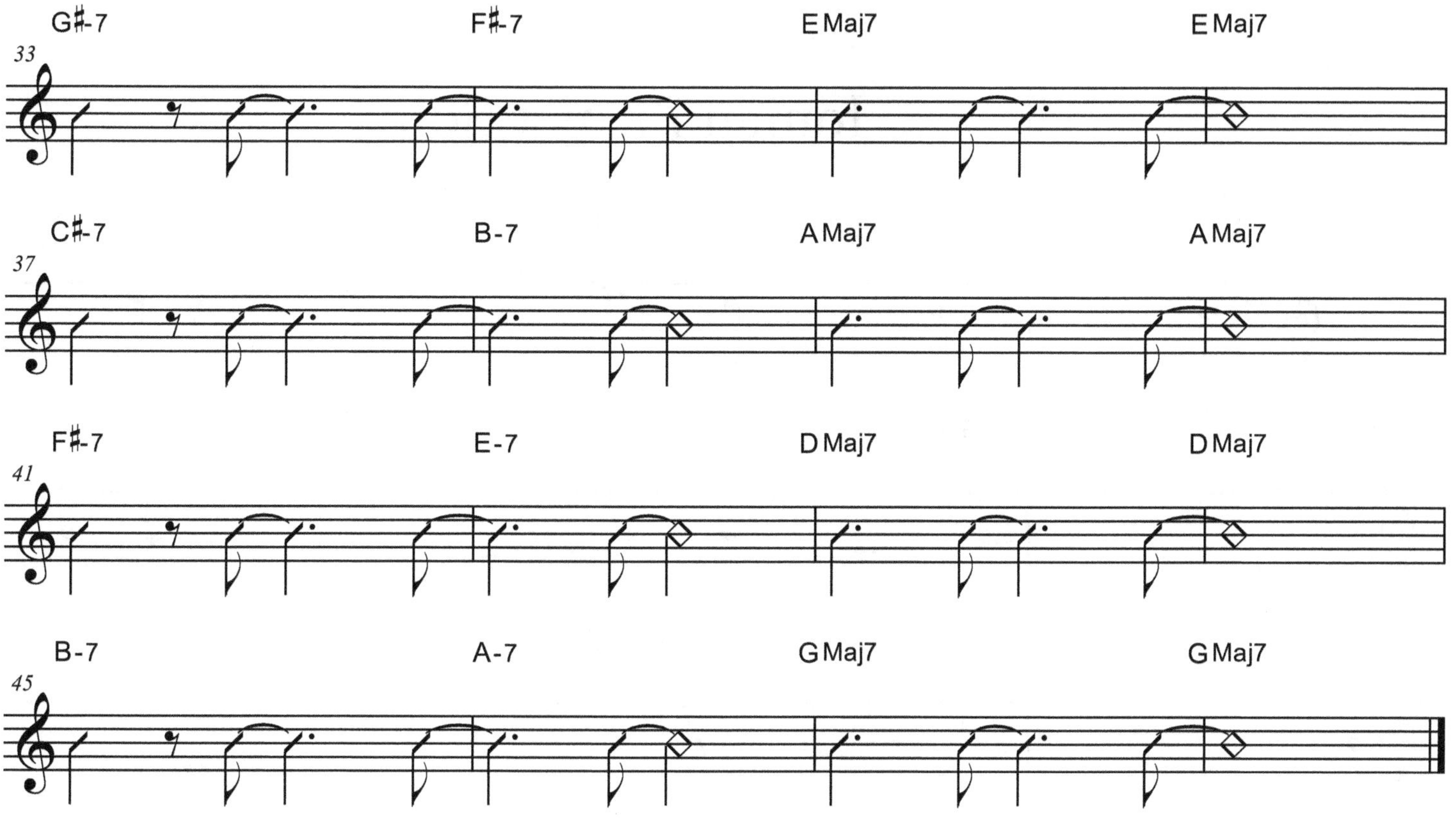
G♯-7
F♯-7
E Maj7
E Maj7
33
C♯-7
B-7
A Maj7
A Maj7
37
F♯-7
E-7
D Maj7
D Maj7
41
B-7
A-7
G Maj7
G Maj7
45

Ionian Primer Solo

Notice the extensive use of tensions as long notes. Remember for a -7 chord 9, 11, and 13 are availabe tensions. For a Major7 chord it's 9, #11 and 13. Remember that each 4 measure group of chords are in one key. Therefore, when you are playing the iii-7 chord for example, in the key of C Major that would be the E-7 and so you would not put a tension 9 on that chord. I haven't put any tension 9's on any chord in this solo. Remember though, it is possible to use this note; I just didn't use it to keep each 4 measure key center using only the notes of the major scale. Also note measure 41 where I use an avoid note ♭6th on a -7 chord, in this case a D natural on an F#-7 chord. Listen for how that note really wants to resolve. Remember you can use avoid notes as long as you resolve them. Also notice the use of rests and long notes in this solo.

Chapter Two

Rhythm Exercise

Single String Exercise

Rhythm Changes Exercise

Modal Jazz Vamp and Solo

Rhythm Primer Exercise 2

SINGLE STRING EXERCISE 2

TREBLE CLEF

A String Only

In C Dorian

F Rhythm Changes Part 1

F Rhythm Changes Part 2

F Rhythm Changes Part 3

F Rhythm Changes Part 4

⊓ = Strum with a downward motion

V = Strum with an upward motion

Dorian Vamp

Strumming

There is a common misconception that you *must* strum down on down beats and up on upbeats. The example above does follow this formula. However, there are many other combinations of up and down strumming patterns you could use for this rhythm that are equally as musical as the one presented above.

Dorian Primer Solo

Notice how repeating rhythmic patterns can set a unifying solo structure.

Notice how many times the 1st measure's rhythm is repeated throughout the solo.

Notice how a simple rhythm repeated can be effective in the last 8 measures.

Notice the use of the 6th degree in measure 29. This note is an available tension with a strong character so it must be used carefully in order for it to be effective.

Chapter Three

Rhythm Exercise

Single String Exercise

Rhythm Changes Exercise

Modal Jazz Vamp and Solo

Rhythm Primer Exercise 3

SINGLE STRING EXERCISE 3

TREBLE CLEF

D String Only

In C Phrygian

Bb Rhythm Changes Part 1

Bb Rhythm Changes Part 2

B♭ Rhythm Changes Part 3

Bb Rhythm Changes Part 4

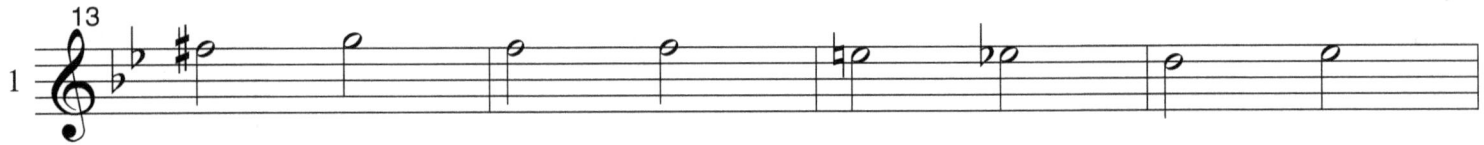

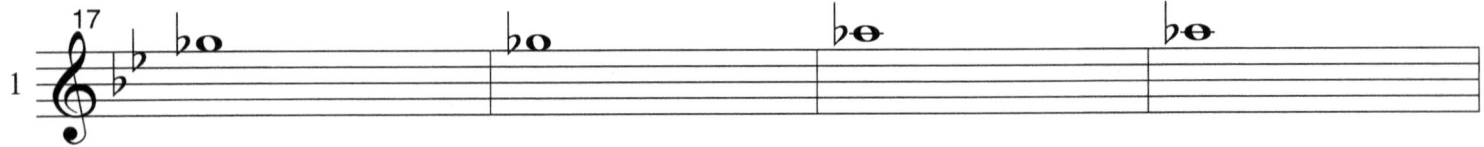

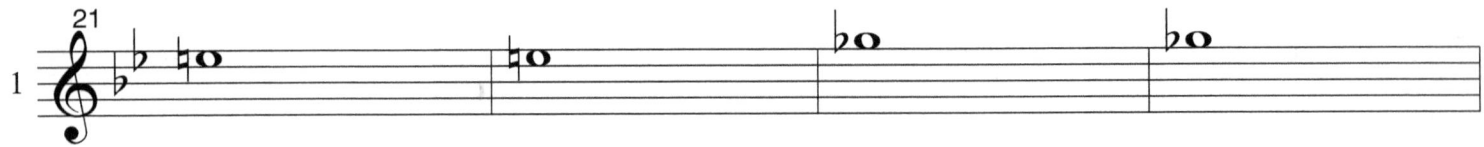

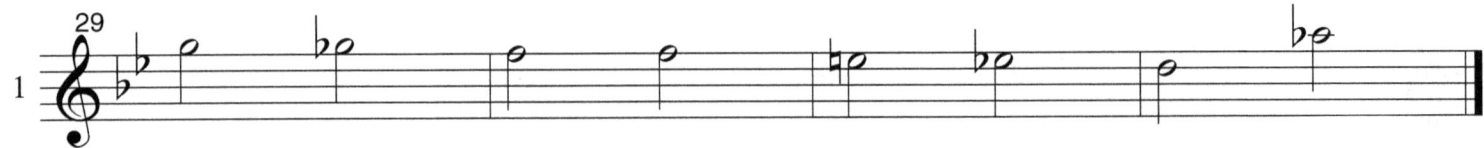

Phrygian Vamp

Phrygian Primer Solo

E-7 G7 FMaj7 E-7 G7 FMaj7
33
A-7 C7 B♭Maj7 A-7 C7 B♭Maj7
37
D-7 F7 E♭Maj7 D-7 F7 E♭Maj7
41
G-7 B♭7 A♭Maj7 G-7 B♭7 A♭Maj7
45

Chapter Four

Rhythm Exercise

Single String Exercise

Rhythm Changes Exercise

Modal Jazz Vamp and Solo

Rhythm Primer Exercise 4

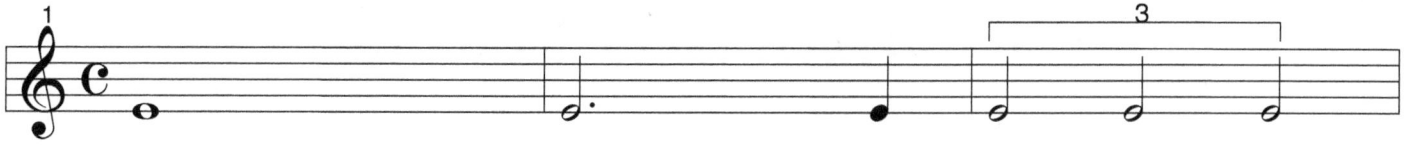

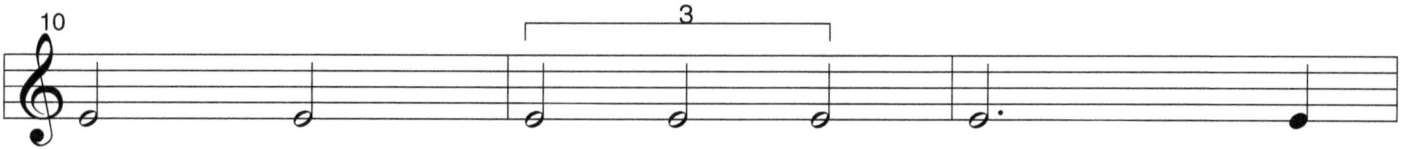

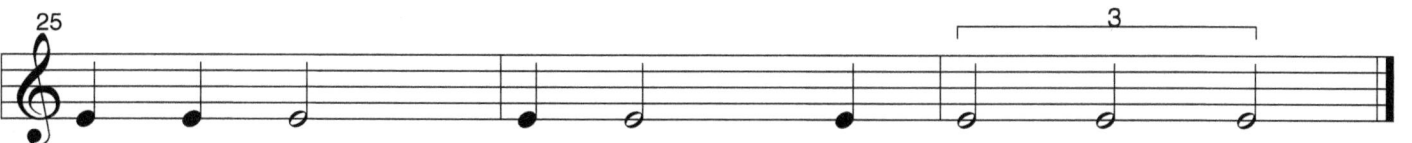

SINGLE STRING EXERCISE 4

TREBLE CLEF

G String Only

In C Lydian

E♭ Rhythm Changes Part 1

E♭ Rhythm Changes Part 2

E♭ Rhythm Changes Part 3

E♭ Rhythm Changes Part 4

$\sqcap$ = Strum with a downward motion

$\vee$ = Strum with an upward motion

Lydian Vamp

C Maj7 $\sqcap$ $\vee$ $\vee$ D 7 $\sqcap$ $\sqcap$ F Maj7   G 7

B♭7   C 7   E♭Maj7   F 7

A♭Maj7   B♭7   D♭Maj7   E♭7

G♭Maj7   A♭7   B Maj7   D♭7

E Maj7   F♯7   A Maj7   B 7

D Maj7   E 7   G Maj7   A 7

Lydian Primer Solo

Notice how many times the ♯4 is use as a long melody note which accents the Lydian sound.

Chapter Five

Rhythm Exercise

Single String Exercise

Rhythm Changes Exercise

Modal Jazz Vamp and Solo

Rhythm Primer Exercise 5

SINGLE STRING EXERCISE 5

TREBLE CLEF

B String Only

In C Mixolydian

Ab Rhythm Changes Part 1

A♭ Rhythm Changes Part 2

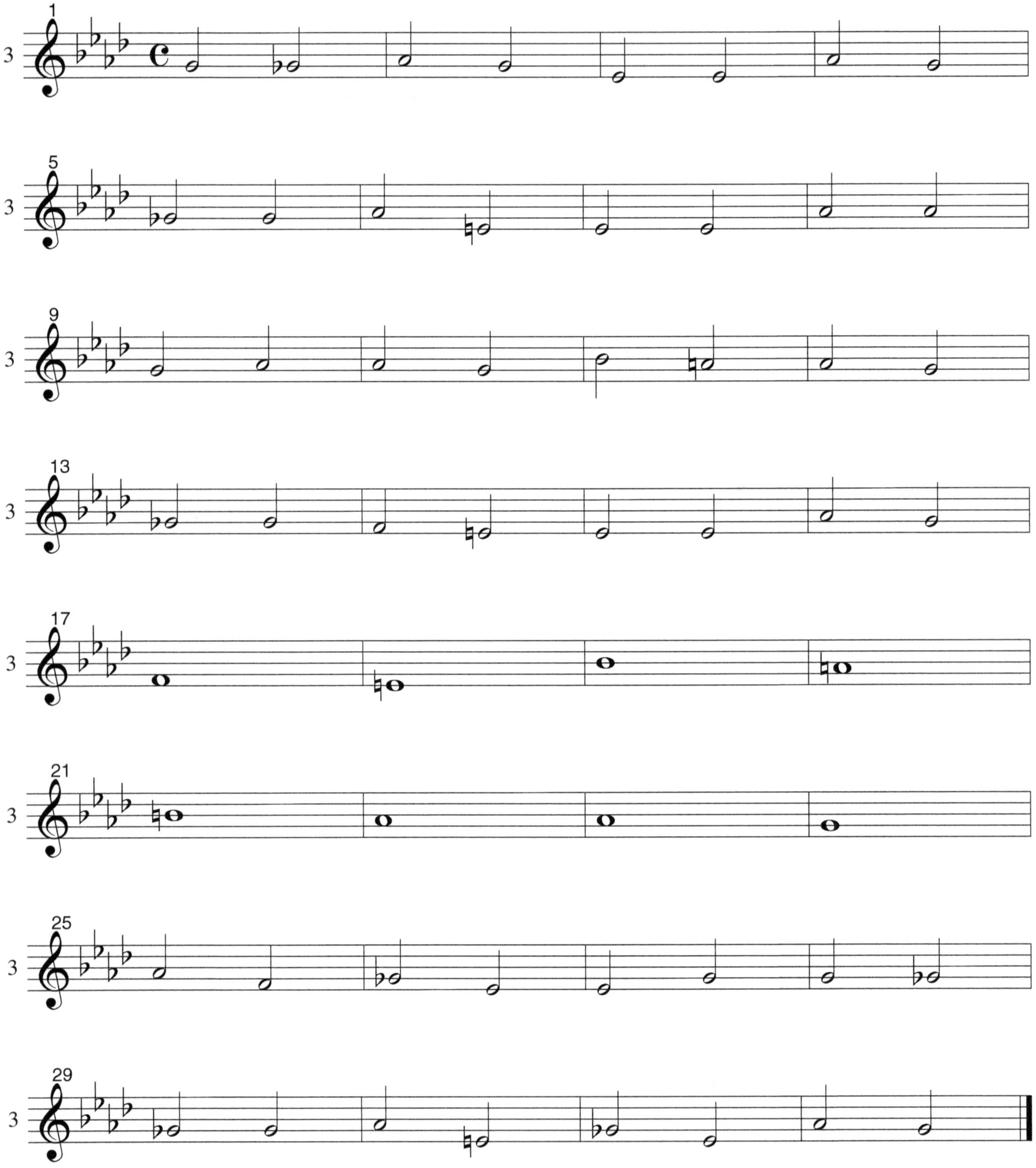

Ab Rhythm Changes Part 3

Ab Rhythm Changes Part 4

Mixolydian Vamp

73

E7

A7

D7

G7

Mixolydian Primer Solo

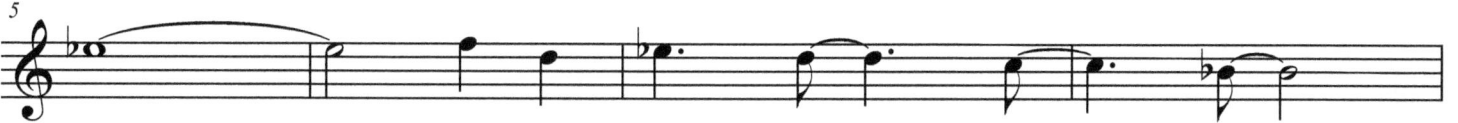

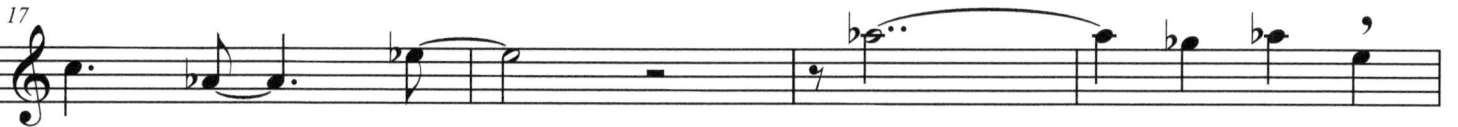

Notice the measures with an '. These notes are approach notes which we will study in depth in the future. In these examples the approach note is a chromatic step above or below the note that follows. Also notice that the note that follows is a chord tone on the new chord. Approaching a chord tone is a typical way that approach notes are used.

Chapter Six

Rhythm Exercise

Single String Exercise

Rhythm Changes Exercise

Modal Jazz Vamp and Solo

Rhythm Primer Exercise 6

SINGLE STRING EXERCISE 6

TREBLE CLEF

High E String Only

In C Aeolian

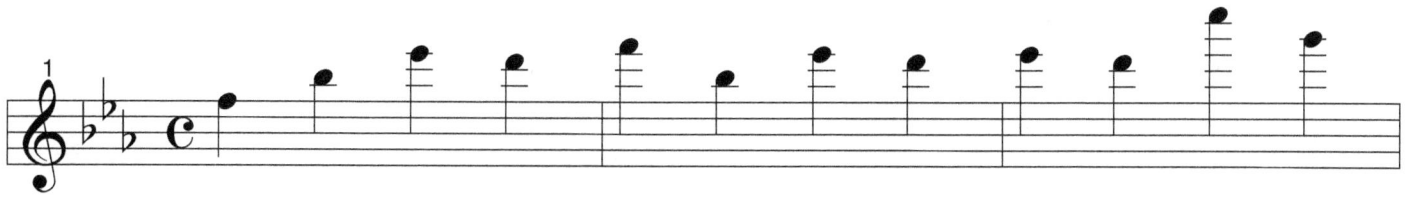

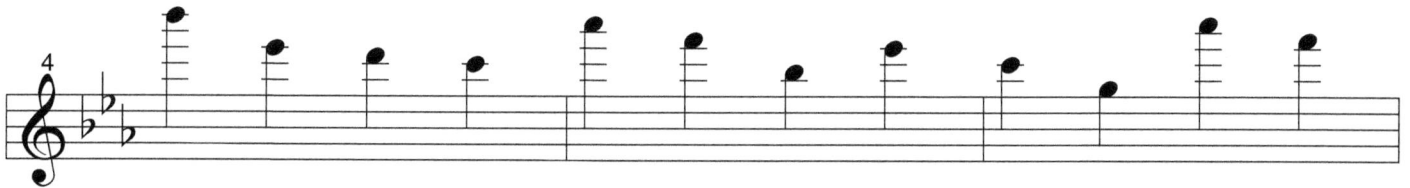

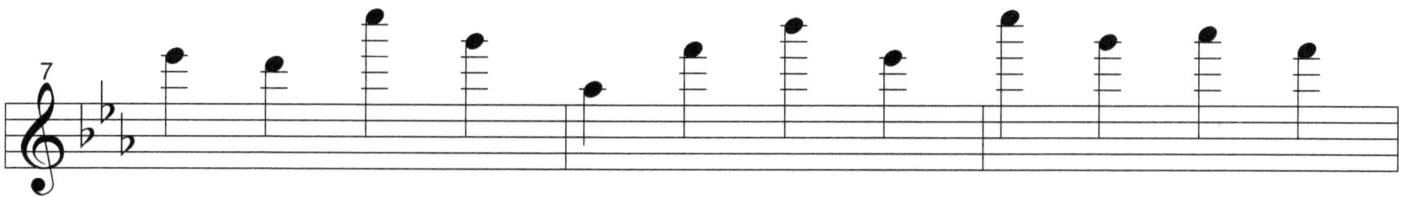

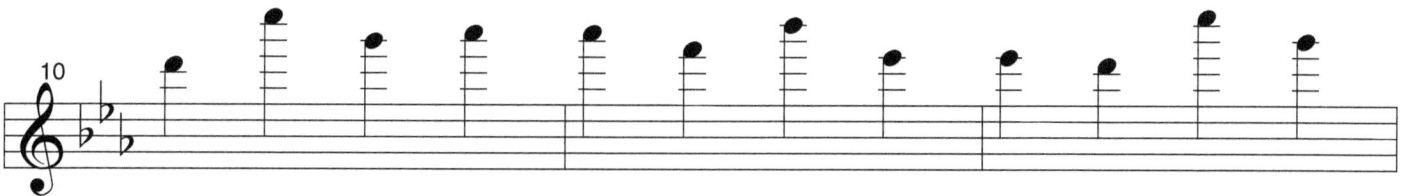

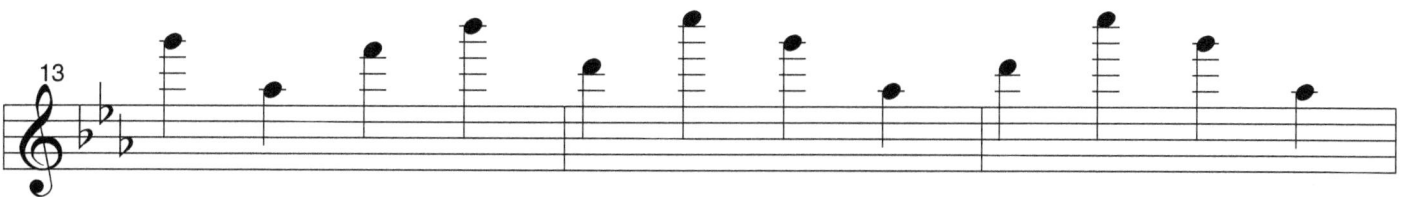

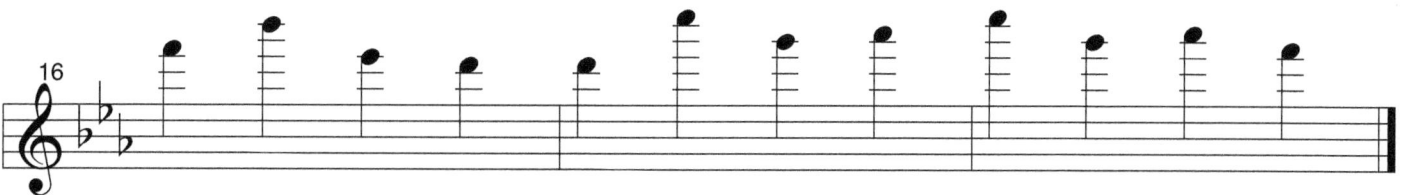

D♭ Rhythm Changes Part 1

D♭ Rhythm Changes Part 2

D♭ Rhythm Changes Part 3

Db Rhythm Changes Part 4

= Strum with a downward motion

= Strum with an upward motion

Aeolian Vamp

Aeolian Primer Solo

The available tensions for a minor chord in an Aeolian situation are tension 9 and 11. Notice how many measures have either the 9th or the 11th as long melody notes. These tensions add more "color" to the solo and make it interesting. Aeolian has the avoid note ♭6th. This means you can play the ♭6th but it will feel like it needs to resolve. Measure 41 is a good example to hear this resolution tendency. Notice how the B♭ wants to resolve to A.

Chapter Seven

Rhythm Exercise

Single String Exercise

Rhythm Changes Exercise

Modal Jazz Vamp and Solo

Rhythm Primer Exercise 7

SINGLE STRING EXERCISE 7

TREBLE CLEF

Low E String Only

In C Locrian

G♭ Rhythm Changes Part 1

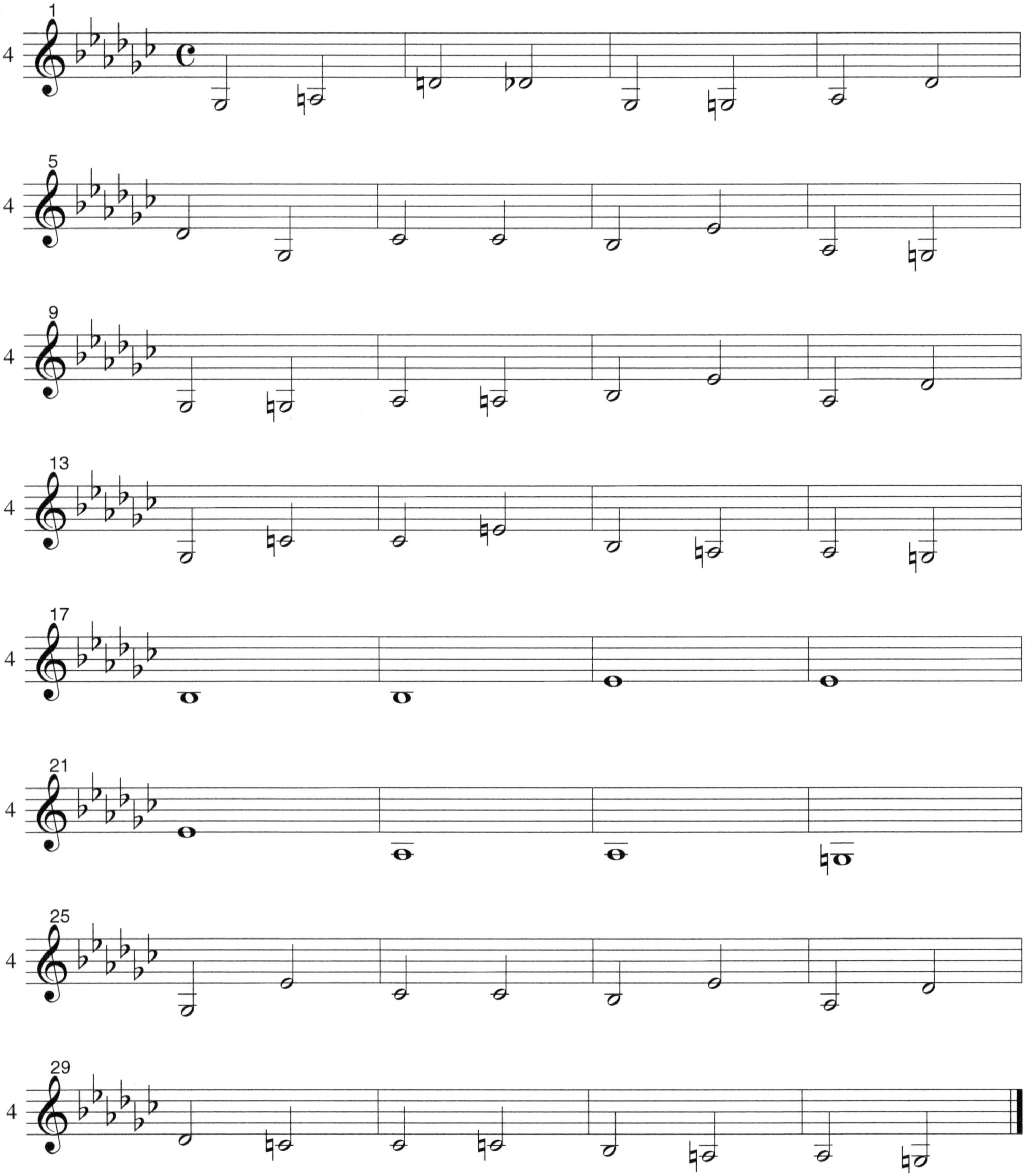

G♭ Rhythm Changes Part 2

Gb Rhythm Changes Part 3

G♭ Rhythm Changes Part 4

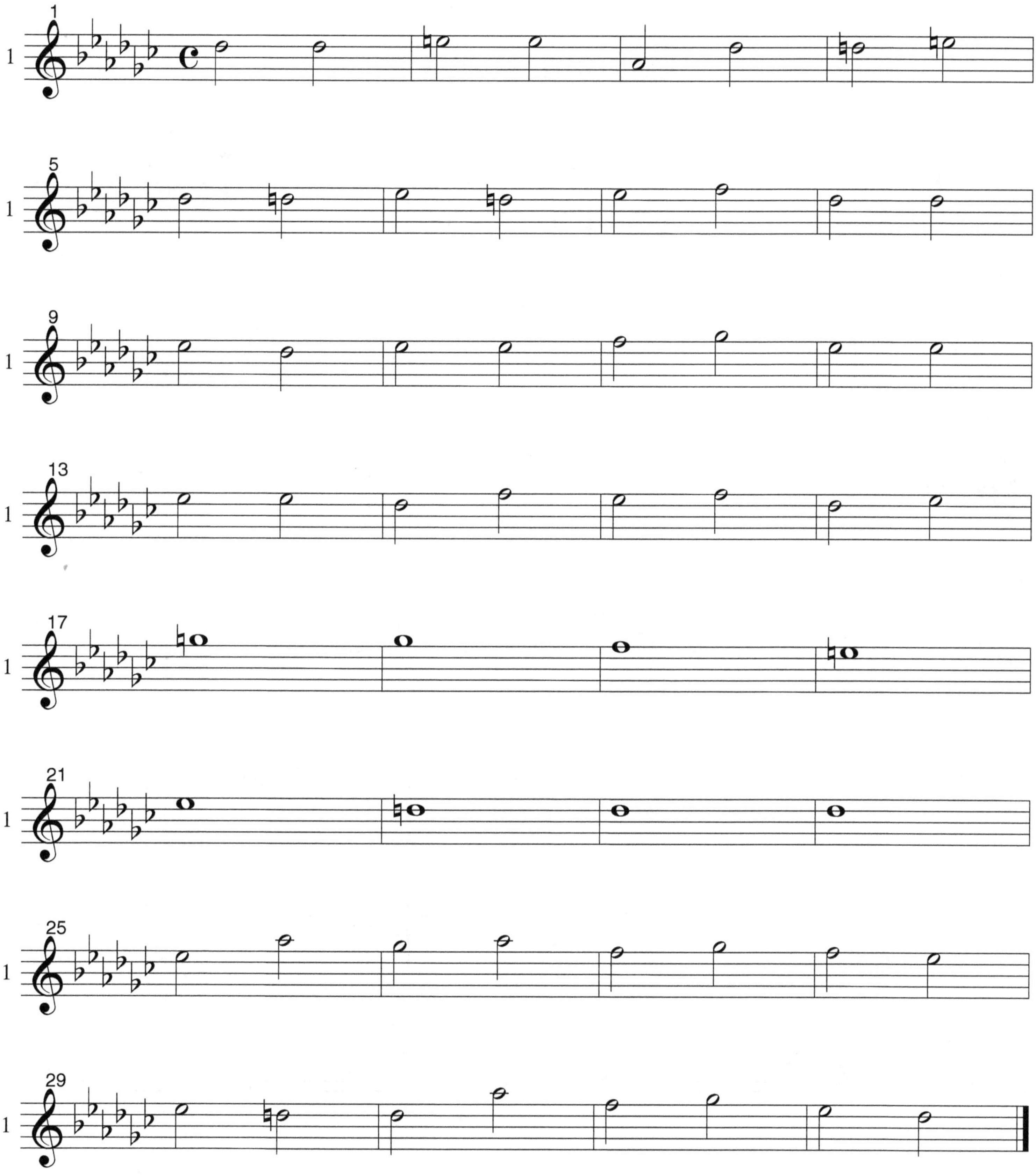

= Strum with a downward motion

= Strum with an upward motion

Locrian Vamp

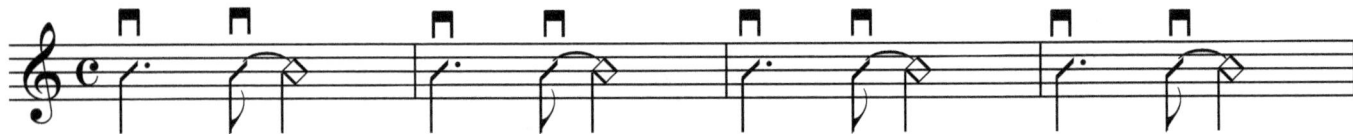

E-7♭5

A-7♭5

D-7♭5

G-7♭5

Locrian Primer Solo

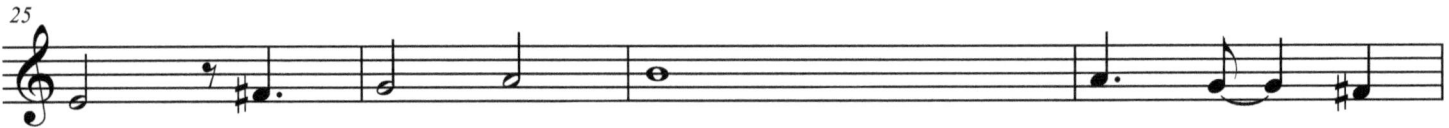

Notice the use of the ♭6th and 11th as long tones. These notes are some of the available tensions commonly used on a -7♭5.

Chapter Eight

Rhythm Exercise

Single String Exercise

Rhythm Changes Exercise

Modal Jazz Vamp and Solo

Rhythm Primer Exercise 8

SINGLE STRING EXERCISE 8

TREBLE CLEF

A String Only

In C Major Pentatonic

B Rhythm Changes Part 1

B Rhythm Changes Part 2

B Rhythm Changes Part 3

B Rhythm Changes Part 4

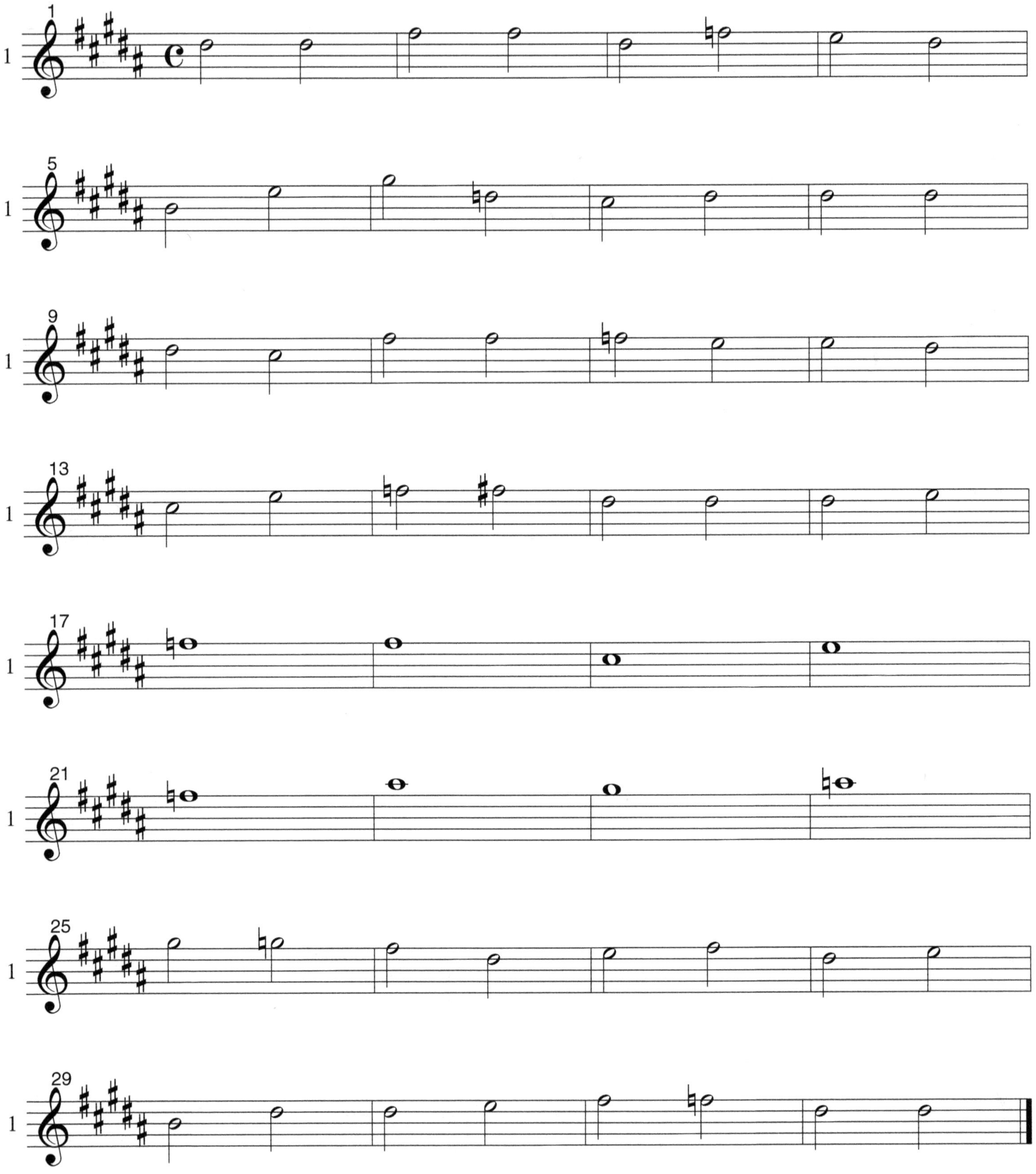

⊓ = Strum with a downward motion

V = Strum with an upward motion

Major Pentatonic Vamp

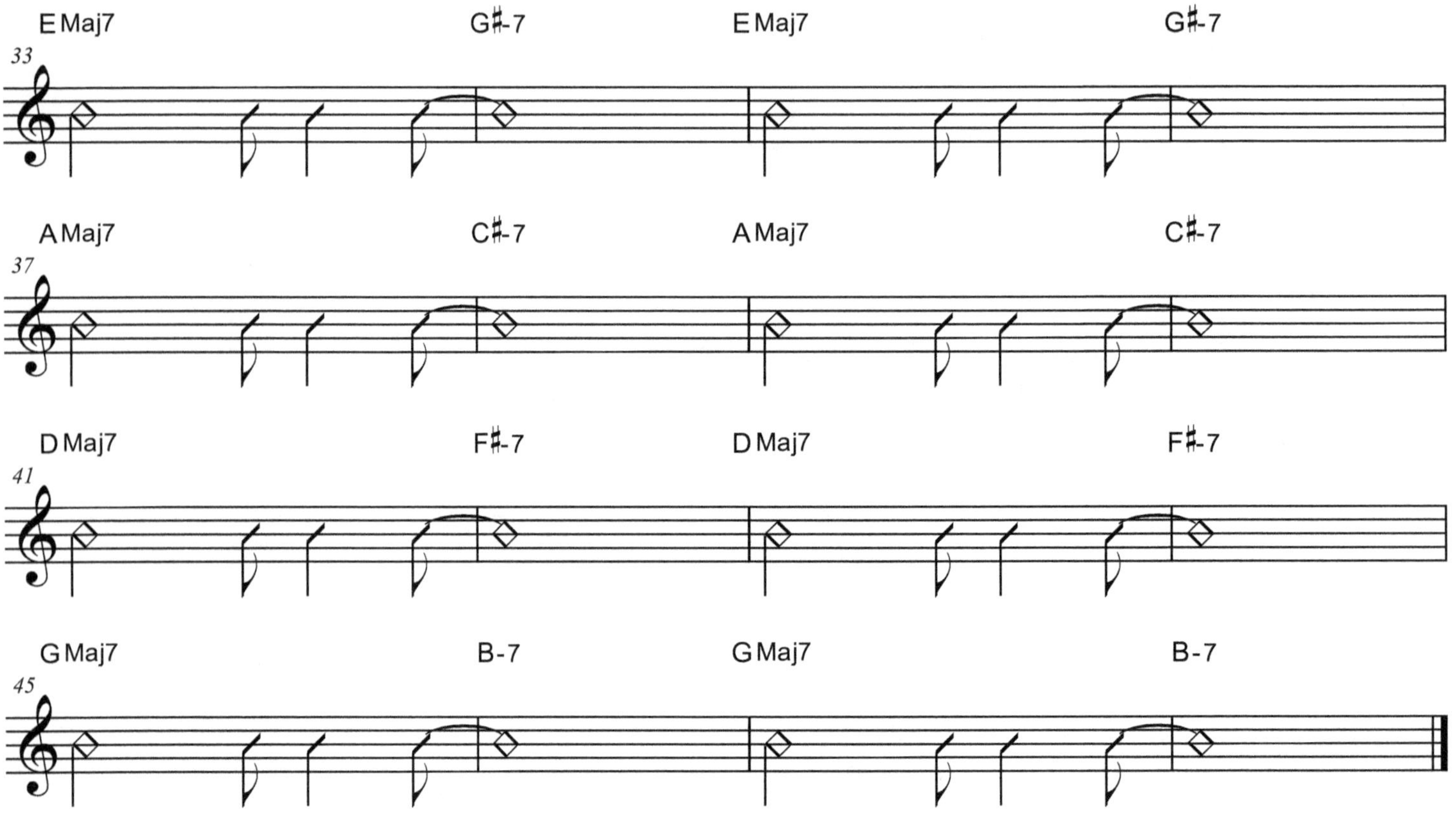
E Maj7 G♯-7 E Maj7 G♯-7
33
A Maj7 C♯-7 A Maj7 C♯-7
37
D Maj7 F♯-7 D Maj7 F♯-7
41
G Maj7 B-7 G Maj7 B-7
45

Major Pentatonic Primer Solo

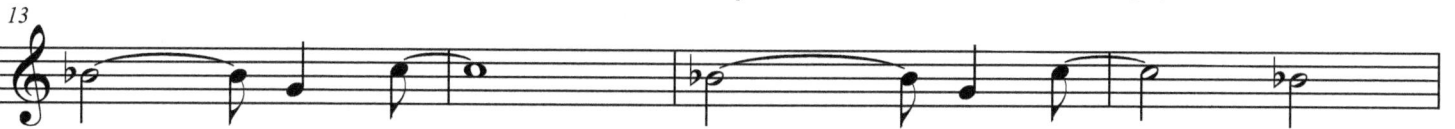

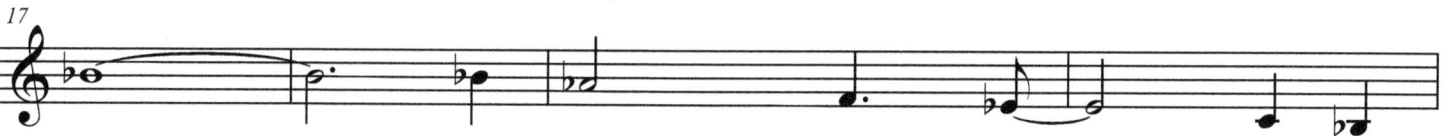

Pentatonic scales are often played in melodic note patterns. These patterns are often called sequences. There are many types of sequences that can be found in almost all music. Measures 13-16 show a sequence that is repeated in a two bar pattern. In this case measures 15-16 are an exact duplication of measures 13-14. You can also move a sequence through other pitches in the scale. You can find examples of this in measures 27-29 and 33-34.

Chapter Nine

Rhythm Exercise

Single String Exercise

Rhythm Changes Exercise

Modal Jazz Vamp and Solo

Rhythm Primer Exercise 9

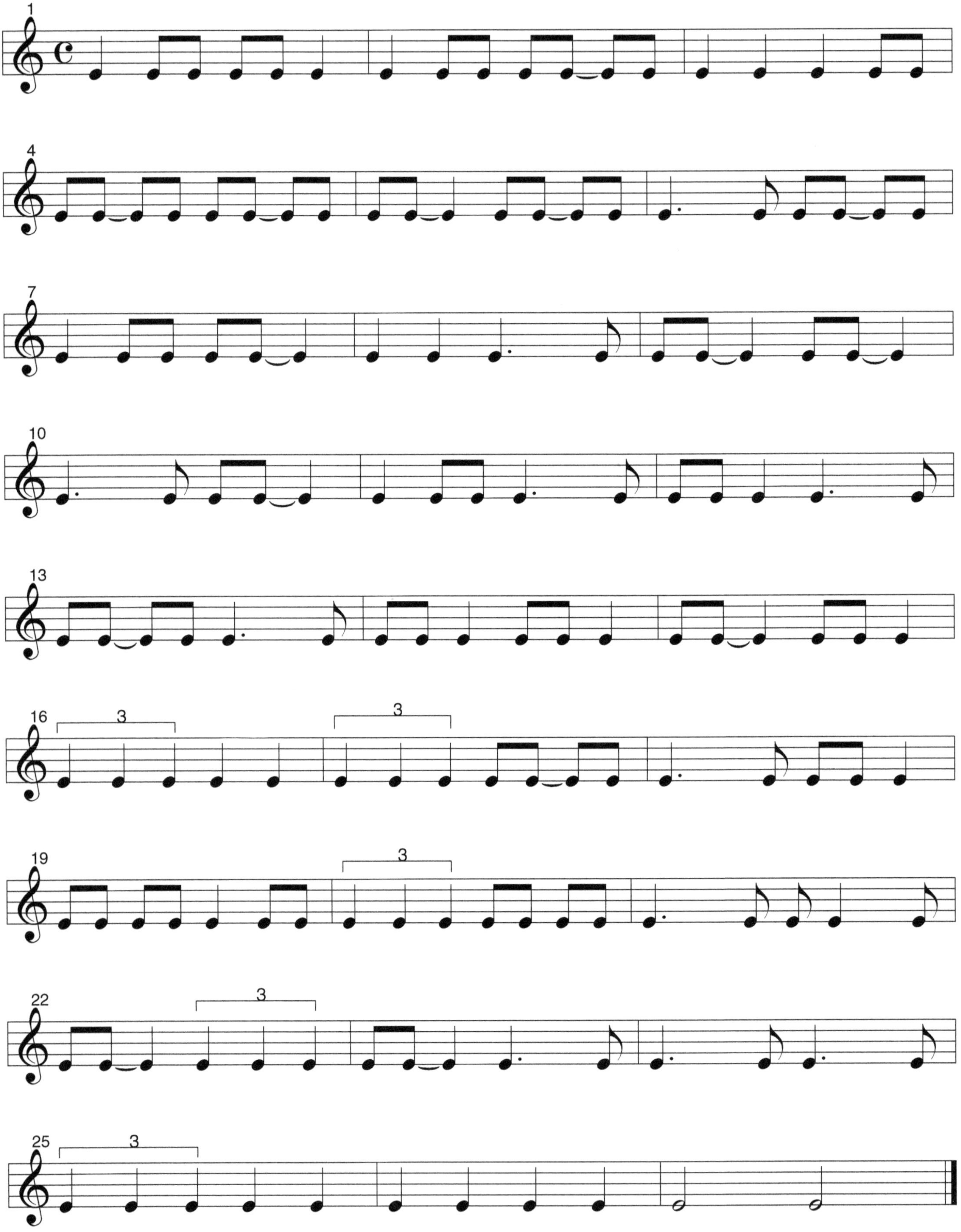

SINGLE STRING EXERCISE 9

TREBLE CLEF

D String Only

Key Of C Minor Pentatonic

E Rhythm Changes Part 1

E Rhythm Changes Part 2

E Rhythm Changes Part 3

E Rhythm Changes Part 4

Minor Pentatonic Vamp

⊓ = Strum with a downward motion

V = Strum with an upward motion

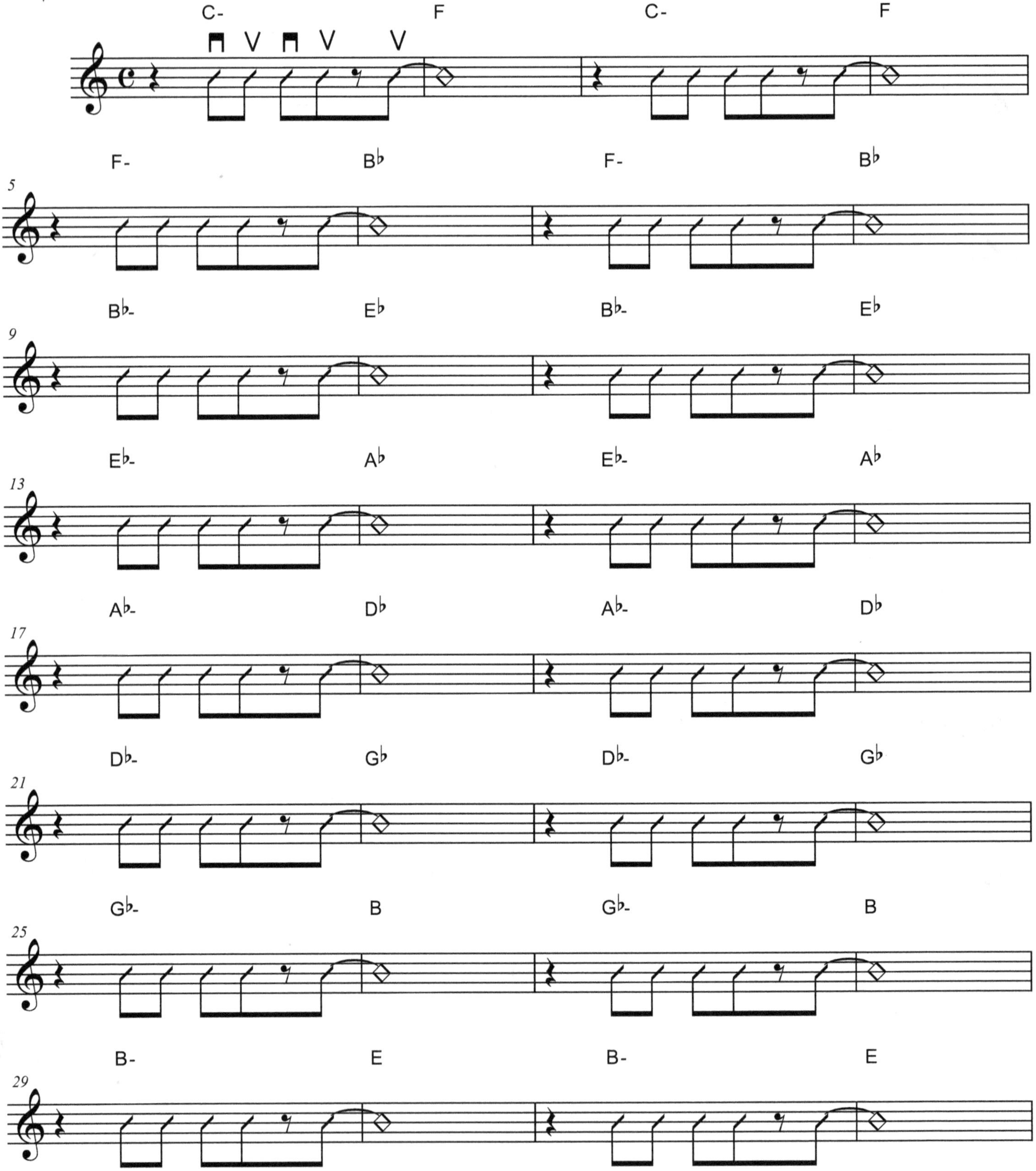

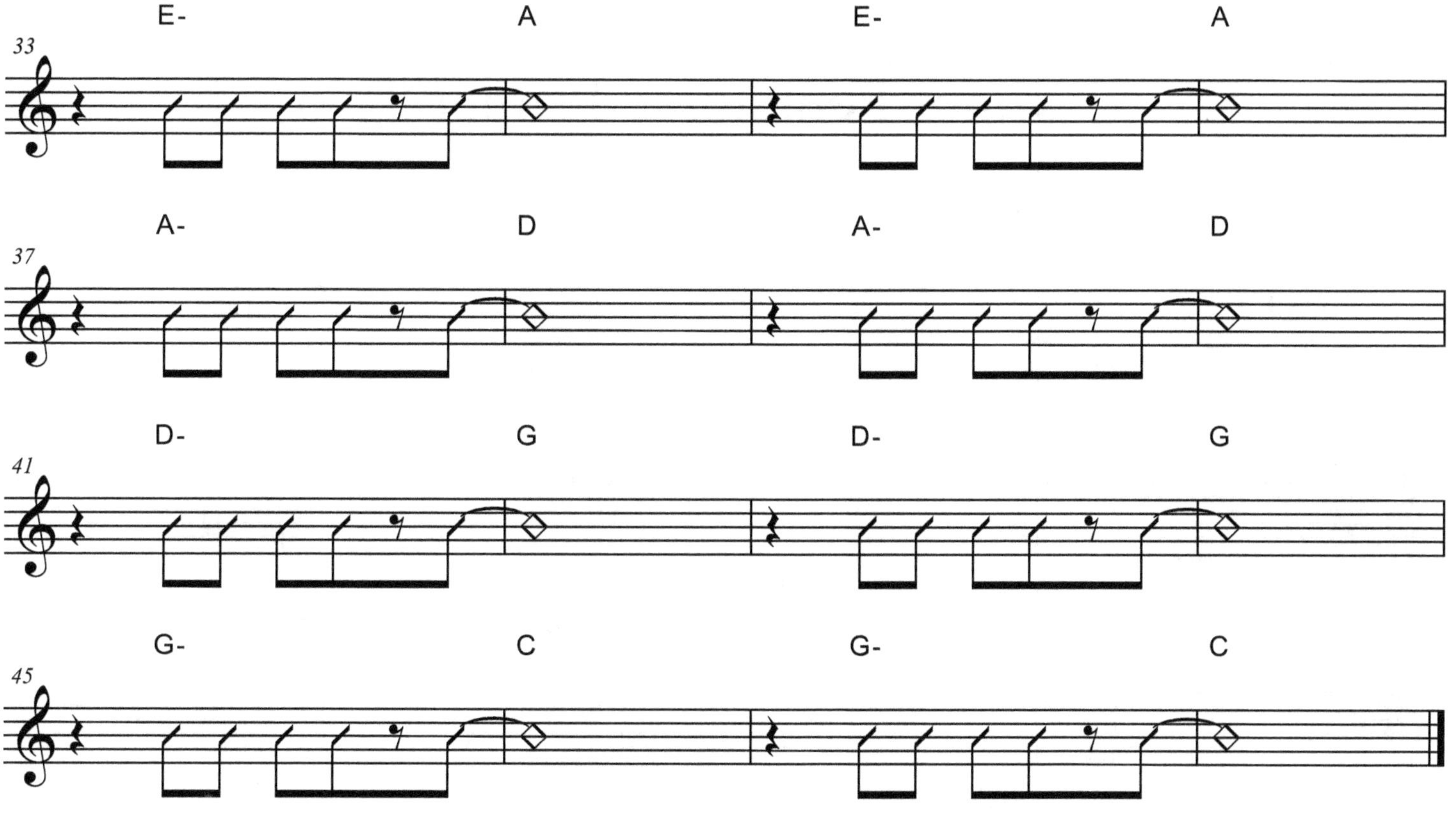
E-
A
E-
A
33
A-
D
A-
D
37
D-
G
D-
G
41
G-
C
G-
C
45

Minor Pentatonic Primer Solo

In the styles that pentatonics are frequently used it is common to repeat a melodic pattern over and over. This sequential pattern can be seen in measures 27-28, 29-32, 33-36, and 45-48.

Chapter Ten

Rhythm Exercise

Single String Exercise

Rhythm Changes Exercise

Modal Jazz Vamp and Solo

Rhythm Primer Exercise 10

SINGLE STRING EXERCISE 10

TREBLE CLEF

G String Only

C Blues Scale

A Rhythm Changes Part 1

A Rhythm Changes Part 2

A Rhythm Changes Part 3

A Rhythm Changes Part 4

⊓ = Strum with a downward motion

∨ = Strum with an upward motion

Blues Vamp

All the 7th chords in the above example can be played as Dominant 9th or Dominant 13th chords. For example, instead of playing C7 you could play C9 or C13. You will learn how to play 8th and 13th chords in the next volume in this series New York Guitar Method Book One.

Blues Primer Solo

Notice the use of chord tones on beat one when the chord changes
Notice the use of the blues scale-C, E$\flat$, F, F$\sharp$, G, B$\flat$
Notice the approach tone in measure 46

Books Available From
Muse Eek Publishing Company

The Bruce Arnold series of instruction books for guitar are the result of 20 years of teaching. Mr. Arnold, who teaches at New York University and Princeton University has listened to the questions and problems of his students, and written fifty books addressing the needs of the beginning to advanced student. Written in a direct, friendly and practical manner, each book is structured in such a way as to enable a student to understand, retain and apply musical information. In short, these books teach.

1st Steps for a Beginning Guitarist
Spiral Bound ISBN 1890944-90-4   Perfect Bound ISBN 1890944-93-9

1st Steps for a Beginning Guitarist is a comprehensive method for guitar students who have no prior musical training. Whether you are playing acoustic, electric or twelve-string guitar, this book will give you the information you need, and trouble shoot the various pitfalls that can hinder the self-taught musician. Includes pictures, videos and audio in the form of midifiles and mp3's.

Chord Workbook for Guitar Volume 1 (2nd edition)
Spiral Bound ISBN 0-9648632-1-9   Perfect Bound ISBN 1890944-50-5

A consistent seller, this book addresses the needs of the beginning through intermediate student. The beginning student will learn chords on the guitar, and a section is also included to help learn the basics of music theory. Progressions are provided to help the student apply these chords to common sequences. The more advanced student will find the reharmonization section to be an invaluable resource of harmonic choices. Information is given through musical notation as well as tablature.

Chord Workbook for Guitar Volume 2 (2nd edition)
Spiral Bound ISBN 0-9648632-3-5   Perfect Bound ISBN 1890944-51-3

This book is the Rosetta Stone of pop/jazz chords, and is geared to the intermediate to advanced student. These are the chords that any serious student bent on a musical career must know. Unlike other books which simply give examples of isolated chords, this unique book provides a comprehensive series of progressions and chord combinations which are immediately applicable to both composition and performance.

Music Theory Workbook for Guitar Series

The worlds most popular instrument, the guitar, is not taught in our public schools. In addition, it is one of the hardest on which to learn the basics of music. As a result, it is frequently difficult for the serious guitarist to get a firm foundation in theory.

Theory Workbook for Guitar Volume 1
Spiral Bound ISBN 0-9648632-4-3   Perfect Bound ISBN 1890944-52-1

This book provides real hands-on application of intervals and chords. A theory section written in concise and easy to understand language prepares the student for all exercises. Worksheets are given that quiz a student about intervals and chord construction using staff notation and guitar tablature. Answers are supplied in the back of the book enabling a student to work without a teacher.

132

Theory Workbook for Guitar Volume 2
Spiral Bound ISBN 0-9648632-5-1   Perfect Bound ISBN 1890944-53-X

This book provides real hands-on application for 22 different scale types. A theory section written in concise and easy to understand language prepares the student for all exercises. Worksheets are given that quiz a student about scale construction using staff notation and guitar tablature. Answers are supplied in the back of the book enabling a student to work without a teacher. Audio files are also available on the muse-eek.com website to facilitate practice and improvisation with all the scales presented.

Rhythm Book Series

These books are a breakthrough in music instruction, using the internet as a teaching tool! Audio files of all the exercises are easily downloaded from the internet.

Rhythm Primer
Spiral Bound ISBN 0-890944-03-3   Perfect Bound ISBN 1890944-59-9

This 61 page book concentrates on all basic rhythms using four rhythmic levels. All examples use one pitch, allowing the student to focus completely on time and rhythm. All exercises can be downloaded from the internet to facilitate learning. See http://www.muse-eek.com for details

Rhythms Volume 1
Spiral Bound ISBN 0-9648632-7-8   Perfect Bound ISBN 1890944-55-6

This 120 page book concentrates on eighth note rhythms and is a thesaurus of rhythmic patterns. All examples use one pitch, allowing the student to focus completely on time and rhythm. All exercises can be downloaded from the internet to facilitate learning. See http://www.muse-eek.com for details.

Rhythms Volume 2
Spiral Bound ISBN 0-9648632-8-6   Perfect Bound ISBN 1890944-56-4

This volume concentrates on sixteenth note rhythms, and is a 108 page thesaurus of rhythmic patterns. All examples use one pitch, allowing the student to focus completely on time and rhythm. All exercises can be downloaded from the internet to facilitate learning. See http://www.muse-eek.com for details.

Rhythms Volume 3
Spiral Bound ISBN 0-890944-04-1   Perfect Bound ISBN 1890944-57-2

This volume concentrates on thirty second note rhythms, and is a 102 page thesaurus of rhythmic patterns. All examples use one pitch, allowing the student to focus completely on time and rhythm. All exercises can be downloaded from the internet to facilitate learning. See http://www.muse-eek.com for details.

Odd Meters Volume 1
Spiral Bound ISBN 0-9648632-9-4   Perfect Bound ISBN 1890944-58-0

This book applies both eighth and sixteenth note rhythms to odd meter combinations. All examples use one pitch, allowing the student to focus completely on time and rhythm. Exercises can be downloaded from the internet to facilitate learning. This 100 page book is an essential sight reading tool.
See http://www.muse-eek.com for details.

Contemporary Rhythms Volume 1
Spiral Bound ISBN 1-890944-27-0   Perfect Bound ISBN 1890944-84-X

This volume concentrates on eight note rhythms and is a thesaurus of rhythmic patterns. Each exercise uses one pitch which allows the student to focus completely on time and rhythm. Exercises use modern innovations common to twentieth century notation, thereby familiarizing the student with the most sophisticated systems likely to be encountered in the course of a musical career. All exercises can be downloaded from the internet to facilitate learning. See http://www.muse-eek.com for details.

Contemporary Rhythms Volume 2
Spiral Bound ISBN 1-890944-28-9   Perfect Bound ISBN 1890944-85-8

This volume concentrates on sixteenth note rhythms and is a thesaurus of rhythmic patterns. Each exercise uses one pitch which allows the student to focus completely on time and rhythm. Exercise use modern innovations common to twentieth century notation, thereby familiarizing the student with the most sophisticated systems likely to be encountered in the course of a musical career. All exercises can be downloaded from the internet to facilitate learning. See http://www.muse-eek.com for details.

Independence Volume 1
Spiral Bound ISBN 1-890944-00-9   Perfect Bound ISBN 1890944-83-1

This 51 page book is designed for pianists, stick and touchstyle guitarists, percussionists and anyone who wishes to develop the rhythmic independence of their hands. This volume concentrates on quarter, eighth and sixteenth note rhythms and is a thesaurus of rhythmic patterns. The exercises in this book gradually incorporate more and more complex rhythmic patterns making it an excellent tool for both the beginning and the advanced student.

Other Guitar Study Aids

Right Hand Technique for Guitar Volume 1
Spiral Bound ISBN 0-9648632-6-X   Perfect Bound ISBN 1890944-54-8

Heres a breakthrough in music instruction, using the internet as a teaching tool! This book gives a concise method for developing right hand technique on the guitar, one of the most overlooked and under-addressed aspects of learning the instrument. The simplest, most basic movements are used to build fatigue-free technique. Exercises can be downloaded from the internet to facilitate learning. See http://www.muse-eek.com for details.

Single String Studies Volume One
Spiral Bound ISBN 1-890944-01-7   Perfect Bound ISBN 1890944-62-9

This book is an excellent learning tool for both the beginner who has no experience reading music on the guitar, and the advanced student looking to improve their ledger line reading and general knowledge of each string of the guitar. Each exercise concentrates the students attention on one string at a time. This allows a familiarity to form between the written pitch and where it can be found on the guitar along with improving ones feel for jumping linearly across the fretboard. Exercises can be downloaded from the internet to facilitate learning. See http://www.muse-eek.com for details.

Single String Studies Volume Two
Spiral Bound ISBN 1-890944-05-X   Perfect Bound ISBN 1890944-64-5

This book is a continuation of Volume One, but using non-diatonic notes. Volume Two helps the intermediate and advanced student improve their ledger line reading and general knowledge of each string of the guitar. Each exercise concentrates the students attention on one string at a time. This allows a familiarity to form between the written pitch and where it can be found on the guitar along with improving ones feel for jumping linearly across the fretboard. Exercises can be downloaded from the internet to facilitate learning. See http://www.muse-eek.com for details.

Single String Studies Volume One (Bass Clef)
Spiral Bound ISBN 1-890944-02-5   Perfect Bound ISBN 1890944-63-7

This book is an excellent learning tool for both the beginner who has no experience reading music on the bass guitar, and the advanced student looking to improve their ledger line reading and general knowledge of each string of the bass. Each exercise concentrates a students attention of one string at a time. This allows a familiarity to form between the written pitch and where it can be found on the bass along with improving ones feel for jumping linearly across the fretboard. Exercises can be downloaded from the internet to facilitate learning. See http://www.muse-eek.com for details.

Single String Studies Volume Two (Bass Clef)
Spiral Bound ISBN 1-890944-06-8   Perfect Bound ISBN 1890944-65-3

This book is a continuation of Volume One, but using non-diatonic notes. Volume Two helps the intermediate and advanced student improve their ledger line reading and general knowledge of each string of the bass. Each exercise concentrates the students attention on one string at a time. This allows a familiarity to form between the written pitch and where it can be found on the bass along with improving ones feel for jumping linearly across the fretboard. Exercises can be downloaded from the internet to facilitate learning. See http://www.muse-eek.com for details.

Guitar Clinic
Spiral Bound ISBN 1-890944-45-9   Perfect Bound ISBN 1890944-86-6

Guitar Clinic contains techniques and exercises Mr. Arnold uses in the clinics and workshops he teaches around the U.S.. Much of the material in this book is culled from Mr. ArnoldÕs educational series, over thirty books in all. The student wishing to expand on his or her studies will find suggestions within the text as to which of Mr. Arnold's books will best serve their specific needs. Topics covered include: how to read music, sight reading, reading rhythms, music theory, chord and scale construction, modal sequencing, approach notes, reharmonization, bass and chord comping, and hexatonic scales.

The Essentials: Chord Charts, Scales, and Lead Patterns for the Guitar
Saddle Stitched (Stapled) ISBN 1-890944-94-7

This book is truly essential to the aspiring guitarist. It includes the most commonly played chords on the guitar in all keys, plus a bonus of the most commonly used scales and lead patterns. You can quickly learn all the chords, scales and lead patterns you need to know to play your favorite songs-and solo over them, too! The Essentials doesn't stop there, though. It also includes chord progressions to help you learn how to chord songs in folk, country, rock, blues and other popular styles. The books contain loads of easy to understand diagrams of chords, scales and lead patterns so you will be up and running in no time!

Sight Singing and Ear Training Series

The world is full of ear training and sight reading books, so why do we need more? This sight singing and ear training series uses a different method of teaching relative pitch sight singing and ear training. The success of this method has been remarkable. Along with a new method of ear training these books also use CDs and the internet as a teaching tool! Audio files of all the exercises are easily downloaded from the internet at www.muse-eek.com By combining interactive audio files with a new approach to ear training a studentÕs progress is limited only by their willingness to practice!

A Fanatic's Guide to Ear Training and Sight Singing
Spiral Bound ISBN 1-890944-19-X   Perfect Bound ISBN 1890944-75-0

This book and CD present a method for developing good pitch recognition through sight singing. This method differs from the myriad of other sight singing books in that it develops the ability to identify and name all twelve pitches within a key center. Through this method a student gains the ability to identify sound based on itÕs relationship to a key and not the relationship of one note to another (i.e. interval training as commonly taught in many texts). All note groupings from one to six notes are presented giving the student a thesaurus of basic note combinations which develops sight singing and note recognition to a level unattainable before this GuideÕs existence.

Key Note Recognition
Spiral Bound ISBN 1-890944-30-3   Perfect Bound ISBN 1890944-77-7

This book and CD present a method for developing the ability to recognize the function of any note against a key. This method is a must for anyone who wishes to sound one note on an instrument or voice and instantly know what key a song is in. Through this method a student gains the ability to identify a sound based on its relationship to a key and not the relationship of one note to another (i.e. interval training as commonly taught in many texts). Key Center Recognition is a definite requirement before proceeding to two note ear training.

LINES Volume One: Sight Reading and Sight Singing Exercises
Spiral Bound ISBN 1-890944-09-2   Perfect Bound ISBN 1890944-76-9

This book can be used for many applications. It is an excellent source for easy half note melodies that a beginner can use to learn how to read music or for sight singing slightly chromatic lines. An intermediate or advanced student will find exercises for multi-voice reading. These exercises can also be used for multi-voice ear training. The book has the added benefit in that all exercises can be heard by downloading the audio files for each example. See http://www.muse-eek.com for details.

LINES Volume Two: Sight Reading and Sight Singing Exercises
Spiral Bound ISBN 1-594899-88-6   Perfect Bound ISBN 1594899-99-1

Recommended for those who have completed volume one, volume two introduces more complex harmonic material. This book can be used for many applications. It is an excellent source for easy quarter note melodies that a beginner can use to learn how to read music or for sight singing slightly chromatic lines. An intermediate or advanced student will find exercises for multi-voice reading. These exercises can also be used for multi-voice ear training. The book has the added benefit in that all exercises can be heard by downloading the audio files for each example. See http://www.muse-eek.com for details.

Ear Training ONE NOTE: Beginning Level
Spiral Bound ISBN 1-890944-12-2   Perfect Bound ISBN 1890944-66-1

This Book and Audio CD presents a new and exciting method for developing relative pitch ear training. It has been used with great success and is now finally available on CD. There are three levels available depending on the student's ability. This beginning level is recommended for students who have little or no music training.

Ear Training ONE NOTE: Intermediate Level
Spiral Bound ISBN 1-890944-13-0   Perfect Bound ISBN 1890944-67-X

This Audio CD and booklet presents a new and exciting method of developing relative pitch ear training. It has been used with great success and is now finally available on CD. This intermediate level is recommended for students who have had some music training but still find their skills need more development.

Ear Training ONE NOTE: Advanced Level
Spiral Bound ISBN 1-890944-14-9   Perfect Bound ISBN 1890944-68-8

This Audio CD and booklet presents a new and exciting method of developing relative pitch ear training. It has been used with great success and is now finally available on CD. There are three levels available depending on the student's ability. This advanced level is recommended for students who have worked with the intermediate level and now wish to perfect their skills.

Ear Training TWO NOTE: Beginning Level Volume One
Spiral Bound ISBN 1-890944-31-9   Perfect Bound ISBN 1890944-69-6

This Book and Audio CD continues the method of developing relative pitch ear training as set forth in the "Ear Training, One Note" series. There are six volumes in the beginning level series. Through practice, the student eventually gains the ability to recognize the key and the names of any two notes played simultaneously. Volume One concentrates on 5ths. Prerequisite: a strong grasp of the One Note method.

Ear Training TWO NOTE: Beginning Level Volume Two
Spiral Bound ISBN 1-890944-32-7   Perfect Bound ISBN 1890944-70-X

This Book and Audio CD continues the method of developing relative pitch ear training as set forth in the "Ear Training, One Note" series. There are six volumes in the beginning level series. Through practice, the student eventually gains the ability to recognize the key and the names of any two notes played simultaneously. Volume Two concentrates on 3rds. Prerequisite: a strong grasp of the One Note method.

Ear Training TWO NOTE: Beginning Level Volume Three
Spiral Bound ISBN 1-890944-33-5   Perfect Bound ISBN 1890944-71-8

This Book and Audio CD continues the method of developing relative pitch ear training as set forth in the "Ear Training, One Note" series. There are six volumes in the beginning level series. Through practice, the student eventually gains the ability to recognize the key and the names of any two notes played simultaneously. Volume Three concentrates on 6ths. Prerequisite: a strong grasp of the One Note method.

Ear Training TWO NOTE: Beginning Level Volume Four
Spiral Bound ISBN 1-890944-34-3   Perfect Bound ISBN 1890944-72-6

This Book and Audio CD continues the method of developing relative pitch ear training as set forth in the "Ear Training, One Note" series. There are six volumes in the beginning level series. Through practice, the student eventually gains the ability to recognize the key and the names of any two notes played simultaneously. Volume Four concentrates on 4ths. Prerequisite: a strong grasp of the One Note method.

Ear Training TWO NOTE: Beginning Level Volume Five
Spiral Bound ISBN 1-890944-35-1   Perfect Bound ISBN 1890944-73-4

This Book and Audio CD continues the method of developing relative pitch ear training as set forth in the "Ear Training, One Note" series. There are six volumes in the beginning level series. Through practice, the student eventually gains the ability to recognize the key and the names of any two notes played simultaneously. Volume Five concentrates on 2nds. Prerequisite: a strong grasp of the One Note method.

Ear Training TWO NOTE: Beginning Level Volume Six
Spiral Bound ISBN 1-890944-36-X   Perfect Bound ISBN 1890944-74-2

This Book and Audio CD continues the method of developing relative pitch ear training as set forth in the "Ear Training, One Note" series. There are six volumes in the beginning level series. Through practice, the student eventually gains the ability to recognize the key and the names of any two notes played simultaneously. Volume Six concentrates on 7ths. Prerequisite: a strong grasp of the One Note method.

Comping Styles Series

This series is built on the progressions found in Chord Workbook Volume One. Each book covers a specific style of music and presents exercises to help a guitarist, bassist or drummer master that style. Audio CDs are also available so a student can play along with each example and really get "into the groove."

Comping Styles for the Guitar Volume Two FUNK
Spiral Bound ISBN 1-890944-07-6   Perfect Bound ISBN 1890944-60-2

This volume teaches a student how to play guitar or piano in a funk style. 36 Progressions are presented: 12 keys of a Major and Minor Blues plus 12 keys of Rhythm Changes A different groove is presented for each exercise giving the student a wide range of funk rhythms to master. An Audio CD is also included so a student can play along with each example and really get "into the groove." The audio CD contains "trio" versions of each exercise with Guitar, Bass and Drums.

Comping Styles for the Bass Volume Two FUNK
Spiral Bound ISBN 1-890944-08-4   Perfect Bound ISBN 1890944-61-0

This volume teaches a student how to play bass in a funk style. 36 Progressions are presented: 12 keys of a Major and Minor Blues plus 12 keys of Rhythm Changes A different groove is presented for each exercise giving the student a wide range of funk rhythms to master. An Audio CD is also included so a student can play along with each example and really get "into the groove." The audio CD contains "trio" versions of each exercise with Guitar, Bass and Drums.

Jazz and Blues Bass Line
Spiral Bound ISBN 1-890944-15-7   Perfect Bound ISBN 1890944-16-5

 This book covers the basics of bass line construction. A theoretical guide to building bass lines is presented along with 36 chord progressions utilizing the twelve keys of a Major and Minor Blues, plus twelve keys of Rhythm Changes. A reharmonization section is also provided which demonstrates how to reharmonize a chord progression on the spot.

Time Series

 The Doing Time series presents a method for contacting, developing and relying on your internal time sense: This series is an excellent resource for any musician who is serious about developing strong internal sense of time. This is particularly useful in any kind of music where the rhythms and time signatures may be very complex or free, and there is no conductor.

THE BIG METRONOME
Spiral Bound ISBN 1-890944-37-8   Perfect Bound ISBN 1890944-82-3

 The Big Metronome is designed to help you develop a better internal sense of time. This is accomplished by requiring you to "feel time" rather than having you rely on the steady click of a metronome. The idea is to slowly wean yourself away from an external device and rely on your internal/natural sense of time. The exercises presented work in conjunction with the three CDs that accompany this book. CD 1 presents the first 13 settings from a traditional metronome 40-66; the second CD contains metronome markings 69-116, and the third CD contains metronome markings 120-208. The first CD gives you a 2 bar count off and a click every measure, the second CD gives you a 2 bar count off and a click every 2 measures, the 3rd CD gives you a 2 bar count off and a click every 4 measures. By presenting all common metronome markings a student can use these 3 CDs as a replacement for a traditional metronome.

Doing Time with the Blues Volume One:
Spiral Bound ISBN 1-890944-17-3   Perfect Bound ISBN 1890944-78-5

 The book and CD presents a method for gaining an internal sense of time thereby eliminating dependence on a metronome. The book presents the basic concept for developing good time and also includes exercises that can be practiced with the CD. The CD provides eight 8 minute tracks at different tempos in which the time is delineated every 2 bars, and with an extra hit every 12 bars to outline the blues form. The student may then use the exercises presented in the book to gain control of their execution or improvise to gain control of their ideas using this bare minimum of time delineation.

Doing Time with the Blues Volume Two:
Spiral Bound ISBN 1-890944-18-1   Perfect Bound ISBN 1890944-79-3

 This is the 2nd volume of a four volume series which presents a method for developing a musicians internal sense of time, thereby eliminating dependence on a metronome. This 2nd volume presents different exercises which further the development of this time sense. This 2nd volume begins to test even a professional level players ability. The CD provides eight 8 minute tracks at different tempos in which the time is delineated every 4 bars with an extra hit every 12 bars to outline the blues form.   New exercises are also included that can be practiced with the CD. This series is an excellent resource for any musician who is serious about developing an internal sense of time.

Doing Time with 32 bars Volume One:
Spiral Bound ISBN 1-890944-22-X   Perfect Bound ISBN Spiral Bound ISBN 1890944-80-7

The book and CD presents a method for gaining an internal sense of time thereby eliminating dependence on a metronome. The book presents the basic concept for developing good time and also includes exercises that can be practiced with the CD. The CD provides eight 8 minute tracks at different tempos in which the time is delineated every 2 bars, with an extra hit every 32 to outline the 32 bar form. The student may then use the exercises presented in the book to gain control of their execution or improvise to gain control of their ideas using this bare minimum of time delineation.

Doing Time with 32 bars Volume Two:
Spiral Bound ISBN 1-890944-23-8   Perfect Bound ISBN Spiral Bound ISBN 1890944-81-5

This is the 2nd volume of a four volume series which presents a method for developing a musicians internal sense of time, thereby eliminating dependence on a metronome.. This 2nd volume presents different exercises which further the development of this time sense. This 2nd volume begins to test even a professional level players ability. The CD provides eight 8 minute tracks at different tempos in which the time is delineated every 4 bars with an extra hit every 32 bars to outline the 32 bar form.   New exercises are also included that can be practiced with the CD. This series is an excellent resource for any musician who is serious about developing an internal sense of time.

Other Workbooks

Music Theory Workbook for All Instruments, Volume 1: Interval and Chord Construction
Spiral Bound ISBN 1594899-51-7   Perfect Bound ISBN 1890944-46-7

This book provides real hands-on application of intervals and chords. A theory section written in concise and easy to understand language prepares the student for all exercises. Worksheets are given that quiz a student about intervals and chord construction using staff notation. Answers are supplied in the back of the book enabling a student to work without a teacher.

Jazz Piano Vocabulary by Roberta Piket, Volume 1: The Major Scale
Spiral Bound ISBN 1594899-51-7   Perfect Bound ISBN 1594899-51-7

This is the 1st volume in a series designed to help the student of jazz piano learn and apply jazz scales by mastering each scale and its uses in improvisation. Each book focuses on a different scale, illustrating the scale in all twelve keys with complete fingerings. Also provided are chords and left hand voicings to match, exercises and études to apply the material to improvising, ideas for further study and listening, and detailed suggestions on how to prace the material. Volume 1 also includes a detailed primer in note reading, basic theory, and rhythmic notation.

Jazz Piano Vocabulary by Roberta Piket, Volume 2: The Dorian Mode
Spiral Bound ISBN 1890944-96-3   Perfect Bound ISBN 1890944-98-X

The 2nd volume in the series, this book focuses on the Dorian scale and applies it to improvising on minor seventh chords. The Dorian scale is presented in all twelve keys with complete fingerings. The book also contains left hand voicings, exercises, many examples, an étude to help apply the material, ideas for further study, an extended discography, and detailed instruction and practice tips.

Jazz Piano Vocabulary by Roberta Piket, Volume 3: The Phrygian Mode
Spiral Bound ISBN 1594899-53-3   Perfect Bound ISBN 1594899-54-1

For students who have covered the basics in Volume 1,2 and 5, this book focuses in the Phrygian and Spanish Phrygian scales. It discusses "modern" jazz chords such as the "Phrygian" chord (susb9). The scale is presented in all 12 keys with fingerings. It also provides a detailed treatise on a modal approach to chord voicings, practice tips and a Phrygian étude.

Jazz Piano Vocabulary by Roberta Piket, Volume 4: The Lydian Mode
Spiral Bound ISBN 1594899-55-X   Perfect Bound ISBN 1594899-56-8

Volume 4 features the Lydian scale in all twelve keys; two octaves up and down with complete piano fingerings. Chords are presented with left hand voicings that work with the scale (along with fingerings) Also included are exercises to develop the concept of melodic phrasing in improvisation, examples of the use of the Lydian scale in the jazz repertoire, and detailed instructions on how to practice the material. Added feature: author can be contacted online if questions arise.

Jazz Piano Vocabulary by Roberta Piket, Volume 5: The Mixolydian Mode
Spiral Bound ISBN 1594899-57-6   Perfect Bound ISBN 1594899-58-4

This book focuses on the Mixolydian scale and applies it to improvising on dominant seventh and dominant seventh sus chords. The scale is presented in all twelve keys with fingerings. The book also contains an introduction to approach notes, an explanation and étude on twelve bar blues form, left hand voicings, exercises, melodic examples, instruction and practice tips.

The New York Guitar Method Book 1
Spiral Bound ISBN 159489-987-8   Perfect Bound ISBN 159489-900-2

This series of books distills several of our previous publications into a method currently in use at New York University for the Summer Guitar Intensive Program. Content is geared towards both the straight ahead player seeking to understand previous styles of playing, or the avant-garde enthusiast looking to expand into uncharted territory. Material concentrates on essential information the student must master in order to become a professional guitarist in the heavily competitive New York City music scene. While the book is set up as a 3 week intensive course of study for NYU, it can also be used as the basis for a regular 15 week semester program, should others wish to use it in that manner. Additional features facilitate its use by teachers as well as students studying on their own. This resource consists of a DVD, two Ear Training CDs, and a Chord Vamps CD, all included in each book.

The New York Guitar Method Book 2
Spiral Bound ISBN 159489-901-0   Perfect Bound ISBN 159489-902-9

This is the second book in our series currently in use at New York University for the Summer Guitar Intensive Program. A continuation of Volume 1, Volume 2 focuses on approach notes and discusses how to apply approaches to jazz lines in order to create the signature sounding lines of bebop through the contemporary sounding lines of the modern masters.

The New York Guitar Method Book 3
Spiral Bound ISBN 159489-903-7   Perfect Bound ISBN 159489-904-5

This is the third book in our series currently in use at New York University for the Summer Guitar Intensive Program. A continuation of Volume 2, Volume 3 focuses on 2 and 3 note structures and how to apply them in improvisation and composition.

The New York Guitar Method Ensemble Book 1
Spiral Bound ISBN 159489-905-3   Perfect Bound ISBN 159489-906-1

This series of books combines many of our previous publications into a method currently in use at New York University for their Summer Guitar Intensive Program. Our Ensemble Method presents a breakthrough approach for teaching guitarists how to sightread. Each chapter has eighth note, sixteenth note, single string, lines, and chord exercises. The book also includes jazz and classical reading études and is an excellent resource for lab/ensemble studies as it contains 3 and 4-part reading examples.

The New York Guitar Method Ensemble Book 2
Spiral Bound ISBN 159489-907-X   Perfect Bound ISBN 159489-908-8

A contuation of Volume One, Volume Two focuses on reading jazz solos that demonstrate the many uses of approach notes as discussed in the accompanying New York Guitar Method Volume 2. The book also includes jazz and classical reading études and is an excellent resource for lab/ensemble studies as it contains 3 and 4-part reading examples.

The New York Guitar Method Ensemble Book 3
Spiral Bound ISBN 159489-909-6   Perfect Bound ISBN 159489-910-X

A contuation of Volume Two, Volume Three focuses on reading jazz solos that highlight the many uses of two and three note pitch class sets as discussed in the accompanying New York Guitar Method Volume 3. The book also includes jazz and classical reading études and is an excellent resource for lab/ensemble studies as it contains 3 and 4-part reading examples.

The New York Guitar Method Primer Book 1
Spiral Bound ISBN 159489-911-8   Perfect Bound ISBN 159489-912-6

This book provides students with an excellent foundation in theory, ear training, chord and scale comprehension on the guitar. It is a prerequisite for entering New York University's Summer Guitar Intensive Program and provides students studying independently with the tools they will need to successfully move on to Primer Book 2.

The New York Guitar Method Primer Book 2
Spiral Bound ISBN 159489-91-0   Perfect Bound ISBN 159489-916-9

This book provides students with an excellent foundation in theory, ear training, chord and scale comprehension on the guitar. It is a prerequisite for entering New York University's Summer Guitar Intensive Program and provides students studying independently with the tools they will need to successfully move on to New York Guitar Method Book 1.

The New York Guitar Method Primer Ensemble Book 2
Spiral Bound ISBN 159489-913-4   Perfect Bound ISBN 159489-914-2

This book is a prerequisite for entering New York University's Summer Guitar Intensive Program and provides students studying independently with the tools they will need to successfully move on to Volume 1. Our Ensemble Method presents a breakthrough approach for teaching guitarist how to sightread. Each chapter has eighth note, sixteenth note, single string, lines, and chord exercises. The book also includes modal jazz vamps and solos and is an excellent resource for lab/ensemble studies as it contains 3 and 4-part reading examples.

E-Books

The Bruce Arnold series of instructional E-books is for the student who wishes to target specific areas of study that are of particular interest. Many of these books are excerpted from other larger texts. The excerpted source is listed for each book. These books are available on-line at www.muse-eek.com as well as at many e-tailers throughout the internet. These books can also be purchased in the traditional book binding format. (See the ISBN number for proper format)

Chord Velocity: Volume One, Learning to switch between chords quickly
E-book ISBN 1-890944-88-2   Traditional Book Binding ISBN 1-890944-97-1

The first hurdle a beginning guitarist encounters is difficulty in switching between chords quickly enough to make a chord progression sound like music. This book provides exercises that help a student gradually increase the speed with which they change chords. Special free audio files are also available on the muse-eek.com website to make practice more productive and fun. Within a few weeks, remarkable improvement can be achieved using this method. This book is excerpted from "1st Steps for a Beginning Guitarist Volume One."

Guitar Technique: Volume One, Learning the basics to fast, clean, accurate and fluid performance skills.
E-book ISBN 1-890944-91-2   Traditional Book Binding ISBN 1-890944-99-8

This book is for both the beginning guitarist or the more experienced guitarist who wishes to improve their technique. All aspects of the physical act of playing the guitar are covered, from how to hold a guitar to the specific way each hand is involved in the playing process. Pictures and videos are provided to help clarify each technique. These pictures and videos are either contained in the book or can be downloaded at www.muse-eek.com This book is excerpted from "1st Steps for a Beginning Guitarist Volume One."

Accompaniment: Volume One, Learning to Play Bass and Chords Simultaneously
E-book ISBN 1-890944-87-4   Traditional Book Binding ISBN 1-890944-96-3

The techniques found within this book are an excellent resource for creating and understanding how to play bass and chords simultaneously in a jazz or blues style. Special attention is paid to understanding how this technique is created, thereby enabling the student to recreate this style with other pieces of music. This book is excerpted from the book "Guitar Clinic."

Beginning Rhythm Studies: Volume One, Learning the basics of reading rhythm and playing in time.
E-book ISBN 1-890944-89-0   Traditional Book Binding 1-890944-98-X

This book covers the basics for anyone wishing to understand or improve their rhythmic abilities. Simple language is used to show the student how to read and play rhythm. Exercises are presented which can accelerate the learning process. Audio examples in the form of midifiles are available on the muse-eek.com website to facilitate learning the correct rhythm in time. This book is excerpted from the book "Rhythm Primer."

www.ingramcontent.com/pod-product-compliance
Lightning Source LLC
Chambersburg PA
CBHW062046090426
42740CB00016B/3031